THE GREAT
DESERTS

FOLCO QUILICI

THE GREAT DESERTS

COLLINS London and Glasgow

Printed in Italy
Rizzoli Editore—Milan

CONTENTS

CHAPTER 1

WHAT
IS A DESERT?

What does the word *Desert* mean to you?

Would you define it as a deserted place—a place without people or any other form of life—a sterile place without plants or water—a barren land of drifting sand and sun-cracked earth and dust storms and gravel, and the dry, open veins of ancient river systems.

Or would you define it as a vast, seemingly endless area of sand—a burning, dry, shriving environment with widely scattered waterholes and patches of green from which man ventures at his peril and outside which only the most highly specialized forms of plant and animal life can survive?

The first definition would be the dictionary one and correct in that sense—a desert is a deserted place. The second definition would be equally accurate and is that of modern usage. A desert is a geographical area defined in terms of temperature and rainfall and the nature of the soil, combinations that give rise to distinctive plant and animal species. By modern definition, therefore, no desert is totally deserted.

Deserts have been broadly defined as areas of the world where the rainfall is less than ten inches a year. It can also be as low as half an inch a year. Deserts are therefore dry places but in some there can be

considerable humidity, although rainfall is slight. These are the so-called fog deserts of coastal areas where there is almost always mist and dampness but very little actual rainfall. In some deserts old river beds hardly ever become wet. In others, sudden heavy rain, or cloudbursts, produce flash floods.

Drought and deluge

Although annual rainfall is a factor taken into account in defining any land area as a desert, average annual rainfall has really very little meaning. For example, a desert area may be literally bone dry for a number of years in succession, then for a year or two it may have periods of very heavy rain or cloudbursts.

It is a notable fact that more people die in the desert from drowning than from thirst, for they are caught unawares by flash floods rushing over the land like a river in spate. Such flash floods cannot be harnessed by man to build up water reserves because of the rapid run-off from the hard ground. They do considerable damage to plant and animal life and to any buildings lying in their path. They are therefore a peril rather than an advantage.

Apart from being the driest places on earth, deserts are also the hottest. The Sahara Desert holds the record

This huge sand dune was shaped by the wind.

GREENLAND

NORTH

AMERICA

COLORADO
DESERT

ATLANTIC

PACIFIC

OCEAN

OCEAN

SOUTH

LURIN
DESERT

AMERICA

ATACAMA
DESERT

*Map of the world showing the
main desert areas.*

ASIA

GOBI DESERT

DASHT-
I-KAVIR
DASHT-
NEFUD I-LUT
NEJD
THAR
DESERT
RUB
AL KHALI

PE

FRICA

KALAHARI
DESERT

PACIFIC

OCEAN

INDIAN

OCEAN

GREAT SANDY
DESERT
AUSTRALIA
GREAT VICTORIA
DESERT

for maximum temperature — 58 degrees Centigrade in the shade. The next highest recorded was 57 degrees Centigrade in Death Valley, California. The desert becomes extremely hot at noon when the sun is at its peak; but after sunset it becomes extremely cold. In the Sahara the night temperature can drop below freezing point. The deserts of Asia have burning summers and freezing winters.

Wind and solitude

In addition to extreme dryness and extremes of temperature, deserts are notable for violent extremes of wind. Since wind is air in motion, caused by changes in temperature, this is not surprising. In the desert the wind blows almost constantly. Wind and sun help to create and extend deserts because they cause the evaporation of water.

Deserts cover about one-fifth of the land surface of the earth and gird it in two belts—one along the Tropic of Cancer and the other along the Tropic of Capricorn. But these areas are not all alike. There are differences between deserts and differences between parts of the same desert. As a result, plant and animal species vary from desert to desert and some deserts have a greater variety of cover and plant life than others and a greater variety of wildlife.

All deserts have one thing in common—solitude. In all of them there are great uninhabited areas. Desert peoples have to live where there is water and vegetation, on the desert fringe or in its scattered green places. They travel from one green place to another but cannot settle in the great voids between. These are the areas of solitude where the only human beings are travellers passing through—like the nomadic Bedouin of the Sahara. A desert has been described as a planet apart—a planet within a planet—the Planet Solitude.

Adaptation to a harsh environment

The desert dweller takes his desert for granted. He has come to terms with his environment; he knows its dangers and its moods and how to deal with them. He has accepted all its challenges of heat and thirst, of life and death, and overcome them. In short, he has adapted.

The plant and animal life of deserts have done the same. Each occupies its special niche, and thrives as well as plants or animals in any other part of the world. Desert animals, for example, have adapted to chronic water shortage by being able to live on little water, by evolving devices to economize body fluids, and to extract water from the driest materials by body chemistry.

Deserts have long been a challenge to men from other environments, just as difficult mountains attract adventurous climbers, or the polar ice intrepid explorers.

Hidden wealth

But men meet the challenge of the desert for other reasons—commercial reasons, or the pursuit of knowledge, or the study of scientific problems.

Geologists search painstakingly for signs of oil, the fossil fuel that makes the wheels of the civilized world keep turning. The agriculturist and the pastoralist seek underground stores of water that can be tapped to grow plants or support livestock. The entomologist looks for insects, the botanist for plants. The anthropologist will travel long distances over dangerous terrain to study the ways of primitive peoples. The ecologist studies the relationships between the highly specialized animals and plants of this harsh environment.

Plants and animals

Although, as we shall see, there are plants and animals in most of the world's deserts, the animals may be mostly hidden from view or difficult for the untrained eye to see. Their lives are dictated largely by temperature. Birds are active in the cool of the morning and evening. Many animals are burrowers because burrowing allows them to escape from the heat—the temperature in a burrow 18 inches deep is much lower than that in the open. Other animals come out only at night.

The wild animals of the desert, like the desert peoples, have come to terms with their environment by high specialization. So, despite the presence of animal life, sometimes in great variety, the traveller can still have the feeling of being completely alone.

Although the majority of people think of deserts as areas composed entirely of sand, this is not always so. Most of them have sandy areas, but a desert may be a rocky plateau, a pebbly plain, a barren waste of gravel or a salt flat glittering in the sun. There are rocky deserts, clay deserts, and deserts with gullies and the dry veins of old rivers.

Heat and lack of rain are characteristic of all of them. By day, the sky may be milky white in the glare of the sun or yellowish brown when the desert winds are blowing hard. Desert sunsets can be among the most beautiful to be seen anywhere in the world and are followed by nights of purple skies studded with brightly shining stars.

The Yucca plant in the "White Sands" desert of New Mexico. The yucca has a well developed root system to tap water and to act as an anchor against the force of the wind.

11

CHAPTER 2

THE DESERT
OF SCORPION MEN

The Kalahari Desert covers 275,000 square miles of South-west Africa, mostly in the western region of Bechuanaland. It is a high depression surrounded by high mountains. The height of the desert above sea level varies from 2,690 to 4,000 feet.

One astonishing feature of this desert is its vegetation, which varies from tough, bleached grass about fifteen inches tall, to low shrubs and scattered thorns and palms. There are even occasional patches of forest, for although the Kalahari has little surface water there is plenty close to the surface to support a variety of plant and animal life.

Along the river beds there are extensive mud flats which become seas or lakes after heavy rain. The surface soil is mainly red sand through which the rain water drains to form a reservoir within reach of plant roots.

A desert in bloom

Acacias grow in great profusion and in many varieties, some of them reaching the size of trees. The long, pointed thorns of these plants are actually leaves tightly rolled to reduce drying by the wind; they still play the part of leaves in gathering the sun's energy.

The acacia roots probe deeply into the red sand and can reach a water table several yards below. They have another root system just under the surface which gathers the moisture from brief rain showers. Even the smallest acacia species, hardly bigger than a shilling, have an extensive root system. In a way they are like icebergs—their greater part is under the surface.

Because of its great areas of vegetation, the Kalahari is actually a desert that blooms and its variety of flowers is rich. Trees, grasses, and shrubs give it something of the appearance of parkland. The eastern areas are more typically desert— long, shifting sand dunes with only a sparse stubble of grass.

A stranger to the Kalahari could quite easily die of thirst because, despite the water close to the surface, permanent waterholes and temporary lakes are widely scattered. In 1849, David Livingstone, accompanied by William C. Oswell, crossed the Kalahari to Lake Ngami. They were the first white men to do so.

The Scorpion men

The Kalahari has a sparse but long established human population: the Bushmen—a primitive Stone Age people, food gatherers and hunters, who lead a nomadic life at subsistence level. The name Bushmen was given to these men by the

A Bushman of the Kalahari in a thorn thicket on the edge of his village.

early Dutch settlers in South Africa.

The Bushmen were once widely distributed over South Africa, but their numbers have been reduced from millions to a few thousand. They were systematically exterminated by Boer trekkers and Dutch settlers, in much the same way as the North American Indians were killed off and for much the same reasons. The settlers wanted land and did not much care how they got it.

Despite spirited defence of their ancestral territory, the Bushmen were progressively eliminated or rendered harmless. Against well-armed white settlers in organized hunting parties they were as helpless as the North American Indians had been.

In the 1960s it was reckoned that people who could be classified as Bushmen numbered not more than 50,000, of whom 30,000 lived in Northern Bechuanaland, 9,000 in the area of Grootfontein and 11,000 in the Northern Native Territories. At least half the surviving Bushmen still lead an independent nomadic existence. Others live in isolated family groups, hunting and gathering food and supplementing this with part-time employment. Yet others work as cattle herders and are virtually bondsmen of white settlers or other Africans.

The primitive life

The modern Bushman, because of a certain amount of hybridization, is nowadays measured against the ancestral type as much by culture and language as by physical appearance, and only the 50,000 or so already mentioned are considered of classical type.

The Kalahari desert, situated in Southern Africa between the Orange River and the Cunene, occupies a great part of Southwest Africa. It is covered by scanty scrub vegetation. Here live a few tribes of Hottentots and Bushmen who scrape a living from meagre resources. They are hunters and food gatherers.

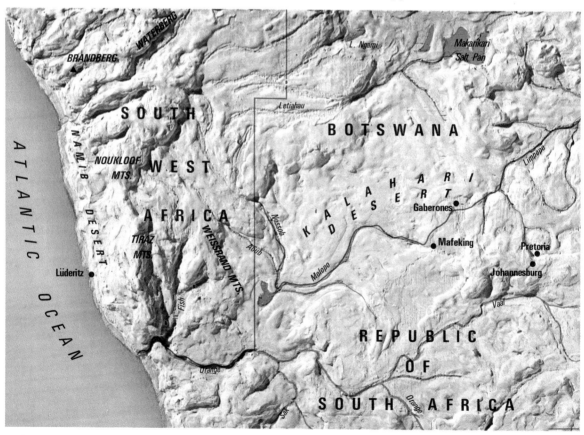

Typical savanna woodland country on the border between the Kalahari Desert and the Republic of South Africa.

In some parts of the Kalahari water cuts deep into the basalt.

Like his ancestors, the present-day Bushman is of low stature, ranging from 4 feet 7 inches to 5 feet 3 inches tall. His skin varies in colour from light yellow to reddish-brown, and wrinkled faces are common. The head is small, the forehead low, and the nose broad. Characteristically, the Bushman has big buttocks, the result of an inward curvature of the lower spine. He has dark, short hair which coils readily into spiral knots.

In their way of life and standard of living, the Kalahari Bushmen are perhaps the most primitive people in the world. Their life is that of Stone Age man. Villages are few, and most Bushmen still lead a nomadic life. The social unit is the family or other closely related group. The groups wander from food supply to food supply, sharing what they gather, helping each other in their hunting, and holding their meagre possessions in common.

Basant rocks of the
Kalahari hollowed and
worn smooth by the
action of the wind.

They have no private property, and there is no private ownership. They trust and are gentle in their dealings with each other.

The language of the Bushmen is unique because of the number of click sounds used in speech, and they are usually referred to as click-speaking people—a characteristic they share with the Hottentots. But not all Bushmen groups speak in exactly the same way: there are variations according to locality just as there are dialects in French, German, Italian or English.

Poison and survival

Making contact with the Kalahari Bushmen can mean a long, arduous journey, because they are few on a vast expanse of desert and their movements are unpredictable. They have few visitors, although in modern times they have been closely studied by anthropologists. People who do visit them have found them gentle and courteous—yet so proud that they are prepared to lead a hard life and risk dying of thirst to retain their freedom.

Their fight for survival against white settler and Bantu is over; their struggle for existence is now against a harsh environment. But they have survived and their numbers are even now increasing. Nowadays, during the worst periods of drought, they are helped by the South African government.

The main weapon of the Bush-man, whether for hunting animals or defending himself against enemies, is still the bow and arrow. He tips his arrows with poison, which he extracts from strophantus bushes and other strychnoid plants. To these vegetable juices he adds snake poisons, spiders and scorpions. The mixture is boiled for a long time until it becomes a gummy paste, which is then rolled into pellets like nuts. The poisonous nuts are fixed to the tips of the arrows just before use. Poison-tipped arrows do not kill instantly. Any animal struck by one dies after long suffering. A gazelle usually takes two hours to die, an antelope about ten, and a giraffe as long as two days.

As a result, the Bushman may have to travel a long distance to catch up with an animal struck by an arrow. He may indeed have to cover a distance of one hundred miles to find it. He has therefore to be an expert in following a spoor. Besides big game Bushmen eat snakes, lizards, and other animals not usually looked upon as food by human beings.

No surrender

The Bantu groups who first clashed with the Bushmen gave them the name *Scorpion Men* because of their use of poisoned arrows. But these arrows were not sufficient to ward off the Bantus any more than they could stem the flood of later white settlements. In these days the Bushmen proved themselves to be fearless warriors. Determined to defend their last remaining lands, which were at that time rich in game, they fought an extremely bitter, violent, and long struggle against the Boers who had settled in the nearby Transvaal.

The proud Bushmen were not prepared to accept servitude. They fought a relentless guerilla war as they retreated, using their poisoned arrows against their enemy and destroying Boer farms when they could. In the end, of course, like other Africans, they were overcome. The advance of the Boers was the deathknell of the Bushmen. Reduced to groups of a few hundred they gradually withdrew into the more impenetrable areas of the Kalahari.

Legend and art

Just as Palaeolithic Man has left his rock paintings on the walls of Altamira Cave in Northern Spain, and in the caves of the Dordogne Valley in France, the Bushmen have left records of their culture in places they once occupied. For hundreds of years they lived in the so-called Bushman Paradise, in the heart of the Pontok mountains, until driven away by war or the depletion of the game herds. The caves in this area are still art galleries of their rock paintings. There is also the famous painting of the *White Lady* of the Brandberg, and the white elephant in the Ameib Cave in the Erongo mountains. Such paintings are also found on exposed rock faces.

Some of their pictures depict the Mantis man, a figure based on the praying mantis—an insect similar to the grasshopper, which preys on

The praying mantis is a sacred creature in Bushman ritual, a creature endowed with magical powers.

Although small in stature and seemingly frail, the Bushman is a strong, active and courageous hunter. During an actual hunt he tips his arrows with poison. Because of this Bushmen have been nicknamed "the scorpion men".

other insects. In Bushman mythology the mantis is endowed with magical powers, and is often represented as a hunter with long, thin legs and wearing a buck's head mask. Many legends have been built around the mantis but no prayer is offered up to it. The Bushmen do not attribute any qualities, good or bad, to supernatural beings; they merely personify the forces of nature, whether beneficial or dangerous. If a mantis alights on a Bushman's body it is allowed to remain there and the man sits perfectly still until the insect flies away.

The moon is also important in Bushman mythology, being a sort of mother deity. It is a symbol of life after death. The old moon disappears; the new moon arrives and goes through its phases. The Bushmen believe that in a similar way they will die and return to life. Such is the moon's symbolic significance.

The nomadic life

No villages are marked on the map of the Kalahari Desert because none exists in a permanent form. Temporary settlements are the rule. What the traveller usually sees is a line of men, women and children carrying all their worldly possessions to another place in the desert —a place where they expect to find water and food. Mothers carry children or firewood on their backs. Women can carry a seventy-pound load without stooping beneath the weight. The men carry arrows, which are their only weapons, and sacks containing their few possessions.

The group comes to a halt at the first spot that gives promise of food and, perhaps, water, and sets about building shelters. The women gather grass and break branches from the

stunted trees. The branches are stuck upright in the ground then bent into an arch; the grass is plaited on top, and tied in place with sinew string. The simple huts are thus completed and a collection of such huts becomes a temporary village. Those who have no shelters simply push a stick into the ground as a marker and leave their possessions beside it.

Among Bushmen there is no formal marriage ceremony. At the age of eleven or twelve the boys and girls find their partners and settle

Two Bushmen children of the Kalahari. Strong family ties and devotion to each other are characteristic of these primitive people of the Kalahari Desert.

down like married couples anywhere.

Seeking and storing water

Like the animals of desert or
semi-desert, the Bushman has to
contend with almost chronic water
shortage. When the waterholes are
full he can drink from them. In
addition, he stores as much as he
can in ostrich egg shells. The water
is scooped up carefully in a small
tortoiseshell, then poured into the
ostrich shells. The hole is then
plugged with a grass stopper, and
the shells are buried in deep caches
as a provision against periods of
prolonged drought. Only when there
is local abundance of water does
the Bushman use it for bathing in.

During periods of drought the
Bushman always carries a drinking
straw. This is a hollow reed fitted
with a grass filter. The Bushman
sticks this into a damp hole in the
sand, or in a dried up river bed, and
sucks water from the ground drop
by drop. Drinking thus requires
almost incredible patience and a
great thirst. Sometimes a Bushman
must suck for many hours and he
will not stop even though his lips
are bleeding from the effort. It takes
much sucking to fill one ostrich
egg shell.

But the Bushman has other
sources of water. Many desert plants
have also to store water to survive.
Their storage organs are thickened
roots, bulbs, tubers and rhizomes —
underground storage organs, con-
serving water for future growth.
Such plants sometimes reach a great
size. There is one in the Kalahari
much exploited by the Bushman, a
spindly vine growing from an underground tuber as big as a football.
The Bushmen take note where these
plants grow and during droughts
seek them out and dig them up.

Young boys are taught to hunt
by elders of the tribe. During their
training they use unfeathered arrows
which are accurate over short distances. Later they use the proper
weapons tipped with poison.

One of the big game animals
hunted by the Bushmen is the gemsbok — a species of oryx in which
both sexes have long, straight,
ringed horns. The gemsbok stands
four feet tall at the shoulder, so it is
about the size of a red deer stag.

Desert of beetles

Another South African desert is
the Namib which stretches up the
west coast and is about one hundred
miles wide. A great mountain range
separates it from the Kalahari to
the east.

The Namib is a much more
extreme desert than the Kalahari. It
has a very low rainfall and is entirely
devoid of plant life, being composed
partly of flat gravel plains, but
mostly of large areas of sand dunes.
Some of the Namib dunes are
among the biggest in the world,
being as high as 500 feet, or even
1,000 feet. These dunes shift with
the wind, their extremities moving
faster than their massive centres so
that they become crescent-shaped
with horns pointing away from the
wind. Such formations are known
as Barchan dunes. Other dunes lie
in rows many miles long.

Perhaps the most fascinating
thing about the Namib desert is its
large variety of beetles. Several
hundred species are found living
among the dunes. They are highly
specialized. Some have spurs or
snowshoe-like structures of hair on
their legs which give them good
traction in the loose sand. Others
are able almost to swim in the sand.
Several species can be found in the
same dune, one living at the top

*Zulu women from a
village on the fertile
plain of Ndebele. The
Bushmen who once
occupied this territory
were driven from it by
Bantu and Zulu in-
vasion.*

where the sand is blown by the wind, another living in the shifting sand on the lee side, and yet another in the more compact sand at the base. These beetles feed upon plant fragments, insects, and even birds, blown there by the wind.

Other animals of the Namib are scorpions, silverfish, spiders, and a variety of reptiles. At the edge of the desert, where the South Atlantic surf throws up new deposits of wet sand, some birds live beside the brackish water at the mouths of rivers that are usually dry.

The Kuru desert of South Africa is noted for a special type of plant known as the Kuru bush. This is a link between the tropical plants of the north and the sub-tropical maquis bush. The Kuru has been described as a desert with a multitude of bushes, each growing in a little desert of its own.

Gold mining, like coal mining, can change the landscape round the workings. Here the debris of a gold mine near the Kalahari has been built up into a tip or heap like a hill.

CHAPTER 3

THE DESERTS
OF ARABIA

Arabia is one of the driest and hottest areas of the world, without lakes, and with rivers that exist only in skeletal form. The rivers can remain dry for years at a time and come to life only when torrents rush down them following a cloudburst or heavy rain. Vast areas are covered with fine sand from limestone and sandstone. The limestone and sandstone are constantly blasted with loose sand blown by the wind. The extremes of temperature between day and night cause the rocks to expand and contract and thus to crack and break. Boulders become fragments and fragments become powder. Scattered fragments and chunks of rock are sand-blasted until they look like fossil sponges.

A photograph taken from one of the American space capsules shows this part of the world in its entirety. The Red Sea appears as a tiny niche between the deserts of Africa and Arabia. The great arid land mass east of the Nile shows as a reddish yellow, fiery glow reaching to the Orient. Viewed from such a height geographic contours are flattened out so that the desert looks like a sheet of yellow sandpaper. Viewed from closer at hand it appears to be an endless waste—a land of cloudless skies devoid of people and vegetation.

This is also the first impression of anyone travelling from the coast— from the sea with its extravaganza of living forms and colour to the desert with its image of death and its seeming absence of plant and animal life. Yet, as with other deserts, the emptiness and the lifelessness are more apparent than real. Life in variety does exist.

The Nefud

The Nefud desert in the north of the Arabian Peninsula is about 400 miles long and 200 miles wide. Here the sand is formed into long ridges with valleys between about ten to twelve miles wide. The Rub'al Khali, or Empty Quarter, lies to the south and is one of the most hostile sandy deserts in the world. It covers about 300,000 square miles. Until 1930 no European had ever crossed it, but today men from many countries explore the area in search of oil beneath the surface. North of the Empty Quarter lies another belt of sand about thirty miles wide and 400 miles long. This stretch is called the Dhana.

The Nefud desert is considered one of the most beautiful in the world because of its colours which vary from bright red in the morning to near white in the glare of the midday sun. Towards evening the red returns, deepening sometimes to the colour of rich wine with a

An aerial view of the fiery heart of the Arabian Desert—its most barren and inhospitable area.

CYPRUS

LEBANON
Beirut

ISRAEL
Jerusalem

Damascus

SYRIA

KURDISTAN

MESOPOTAMIA

Tigris

Baghdad

IRAQ

Euphrates

SINAI

Aqaba

JORDAN

NEFUD

SAUDI

HEJAZ

ARABIA

Jidda

Mecca

NEUTRAL
TERRITORY

Basra

Abadan

KUWAIT

Haft Kel

IRAN

Yezd

Shiraz

PERSIAN

GULF

QATAR

Doha

TRUCIAL STATES

CASPIAN
SEA

Shirvan

ELBURZ MOUNTAINS

KHOR

Tehran

DASHT-I-KAVIR
(SALT DESERT)

MUSCAT
and
OMAN

GUL

EGYPT

RED

SEA

RUB AL KHALI

MUSCAT and OMAN

SUDAN

Riyadh

Asmara

YEMEN

Sana

ETHIOPIA

SOUTH
YEMEN

HADHRAMAUT

Aden

Much of the Arabian peninsula is desert. The largest, the Rub al Khali, is one of the most hostile deserts in the world. It extends west and north to the Hejaz and the Nefud.

texture of velvet. The many coloured sandstones of which the Nefud is composed give it this brilliant effect.

Arabia is made up of many deserts stretching from the arid lands of Jordan to those of Iraq, from Saudi Arabia and the Persian Gulf up to Kuwait. North and east of this lie the deserts of Turkestan, Afghanistan and India. The gateway from the Mediterranean to the deserts of Arabia is through the great *Hollow* of the Jordan, called Goghoz.

24

R A B I A N

S E A

The Jordan Hollow

In the Jordan Hollow, summer temperatures of over 49 degrees Centigrade are the rule. From its borders to its interior this is a harsh environment, yet it is here that man has defined the hostility of nature in a singular way. In the furnace of the Jordanian desert he has built fabulous castles, gardens and fountains. Here in one of the most classic of deserts, in a land of absolute solitude, we find fairy-tale edifices, which, though not well-known, are among the most interesting and enduring examples of medieval Islamic architecture.

During the seventh century the Caliphs, or successors of the prophet Mohammed, built these castles, gardens and fountains. They were the masters of one of the greatest empires in the world—an empire stretching from Persia to Morocco. Arab conquest had taken over the old Roman Empire and even Spain came under their rule. The conquerors were however also creative. They absorbed the best influences of Greco-Byzantine culture. This was the period of the great blossoming of literature, art and science in the Moslem world, one of the abiding landmarks of history.

It was during this exciting, creative period that the caliphs of the First Dynasty built their incredible castles in the middle of the desert. Why they built them in such places nobody knows. Years of neglect have brought ruin to these amazing memorials to a period of splendour, and few people know of their existence. Day after day the remains of at least six palaces of this epoch continue to crumble. They are remote, almost forgotten, and no roads lead to them. The traveller comes upon them suddenly, unexpectedly, for their colour blends with the surrounding desert and they are difficult to see until one is quite close to them.

A visit to castles such as Mushatta, Quasr, Kharrna, and Qasr el Azraq brings home to one how the will of man, in this case the Arab,

An Islamic symbol inscribed with the words of the faith: "There is no God but Allah: Mohammed is his prophet."

A Moslem rosary with its thirty-three beads.

This canopy, in the form of a pyramid, is preserved in a museum in Damascus, Syria. It was originally mounted on the "camel of the king" at the head of a royal caravan on pilgrimage across the Arabian desert to Mecca.

munities, man is not specially well adapted to survive in desert conditions. This applies as much to Arabs as to anyone else. But desert peoples have contrived to overcome the difficulties and the dangers, some by going about naked like the Bushmen of the Kalahari, and others by swathing themselves in clothing. But they all need water to replace body fluids lost in keeping cool. Starker Leopold has deftly summed up how desert temperatures affect human beings:

"Man was never intended for an arid existence. Strand a healthy human adult in the middle of a desert, without water, on the morning of a hot summer day, and he will experience no instant discomfort. After an hour he will have lost up to a quart of salty water by perspiring, and will be very thirsty. By mid-afternoon, with his body's water-cooling mechanism working hard to throw off heat, his weight will be down twelve to eighteen pounds and he will be weak. By nightfall, if the temperature during the day has been 49 degrees Centigrade, he may well be dead, but if the temperature has gone only to 43 degrees Centigrade in the shade he has a life expectancy of one more such day. Even if he is given a daily ration of a gallon of water instead of none at all, the sun will kill him within a week."

Heart of Islam

From the sands of the Hejaz desert in Saudi Arabia rises the city of Mecca, the religious heart of Islam. Here, in the year 570, Mohammed, the prophet of Islam, was born. The word Islam means submission—submission to the will of God, or Allah. Mohammed, after early struggles, when he was scoffed at as Jesus was in his day, soon

can fight a winning battle against even the harshest and most hostile environment. The sand, the rocks, and the solitude of the Arabian desert do not intimidate the proud Arabs. The plains of Arabia, like the deserts of Africa, have their natural oases where the green palms are fed by subterranean springs, but there are also oases built by the Arabs. Here, instead of villages or settlements, one will find a solitary building, a symbol of determination, proof that even an individual can defeat the desert and find a living in the midst of a sea of sand.

Keeping cool

Whether he lives alone or in com-

gained a large following. There are now 500,000,000 Moslems in the world.

Only Moslems are permitted to visit the holy city and any non-Moslem caught there may be killed. Some non-Moslems have managed, by disguise or other subterfuge, to visit it and have brought back descriptions of their adventures. Today Mecca is linked with its port Jidda, on the Red Sea, by a tarmac road which was built in 1943. At one point on this road stand two pillars marking the point past which no non-Moslem is allowed to go. There are similar markers on other routes to the city.

Over the centuries caravans of pilgrims have travelled across the desert to Mecca, sometimes with as many as 20,000 camels in a group. One famous pilgrimage started at Damascus and slowly made its way through the Syrian and Arabian deserts for 1200 miles before reaching Mecca. The entire trip had to be made in forty days because the camel owners would lose money if it took longer. The journey was difficult, rests were infrequent, and many camels died along the way. Some of the wealthier Moslems were carried on litters, and had servants with them to look after them. But time has changed methods of travel across the desert as it changes everything else. Now-

Entrance to the Castle of Omayad in Damascus, Syria. The architecture copies the style of the castles built in the Jordan desert by this king of Islam.

adays, pilgrimages to Mecca can be made by plane.

No matter how the pilgrim travels, the time of the pilgrimage is fixed. It begins on the seventh day of the last month of the Moslem year, this being the day laid down by the Koran. Whether the journey across the desert is made by plane or bus, or truck, the pilgrims have to camp around the city of Mecca. The number grows larger year by year. Up to a century ago a few thousand could be expected; today they exceed two millions. The city of Mecca could not possibly accommodate such a large number of extra people, so they have to camp out on the desert sand beyond the city walls.

Although jet flights have largely displaced the camel on long pilgrimages, and although many Moslems stay in air-conditioned hotels in the nearby port of Jidda, the ritual to be observed by pilgrims has not changed at all. Once he has arrived in Mecca the pilgrim wraps himself in two lengths of seamless white cloth, casting aside for the time being his desert robes or his western-style suit. The same ritual is followed by all Moslems from the richest to the poorest.

The ritual begins with a gathering of the faithful around the Great Mosque standing in the square between the Low city and the High city. In the inner enclosure is located the Kaaba, the repository of the Black Stone, which, according to Moslem tradition, was given to Abraham by the Angel Gabriel. Ritual requires the pilgrim to pass seven times round the Kaaba and touch the black stone. The Kaaba, with its sacred stone, is the supreme symbol of Islam.

After the ritual of the Kaaba the pilgrims have to race round two hills near the outskirts of the city.

On the second day they walk to the hill of Arafat where they spend the night in prayer. Then they go on to Mina, another holy place, where they enact the Rite of the Stones. This is a symbolic act: the pilgrims throw pebbles in the sand in commemoration of Abraham who hurled stones during his temptation by Satan. Finally, at night, a lamb is sacrificed in honour of Allah. Thousands of lambs are slaughtered in the desert, in the streets of the city, and elsewhere. The meat is given to the poor and any that is left over is carried away and buried in the desert sands by bulldozers.

From Mecca the creed of Islam, as set forth in the Koran, has spread its roots wide—from Morocco in the west to the Philippines in the Far East. But wherever they live, the faithful look upon this city in the Arabian desert as the source of their spiritual life. Their faith is absolute. Every believer throughout this great religious empire, which extends from the Atlantic to the Pacific, kneels in prayer five times a day. Each turns his face towards that strip of sand and rocks that protects and encircles Mecca. Arabia is the Moslem's promised land and between its two deserts, the Hejaz and the Nefud, beats the "burning heart" of Islam.

Land in transition

Long before the days of the camel caravans and the pilgrimage to Mecca, long before the time of Abraham, long before man appeared on the scene at all, it may be that the whole Arabian Peninsula enjoyed a more favourable climate than it does today. There is some evidence of this from the shapes of water courses which could hardly have been formed under present conditions.

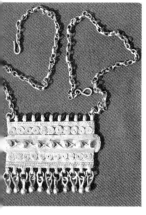

Silver jewellery belonging to a nomad woman of the Arabian desert.

From the time when men first lived in Arabia there was a distinction between the Arabs of the north and the Arabs of the south. This may have been due partly to the fact that the southern Arabs lived in cities, while most of those who lived in the north were nomads, although some mixing had already taken place even before the time of Mohammed.

The Hejaz is a land in transition— of growing commercial exchange between the south (rich in tobacco, coffee and incense), and the Levant. The Nefud is and has been from the beginning of recorded time a land of shepherds and nomads. The people of the Hejaz, steeped in commerce and more in touch with outside influences, show a readiness to compromise and might be described as non-conformists.

In the Nefud, on the other hand, even the poorest Bedouins and nomads in the most poverty-stricken villages, are proud and unbending in their outlook. These are the descendants of the ancient dwellers of the interior who attacked from the Nefud the wealthy caravans of the Hejaz. In these far off days entire tribes of plunderers mounted on swift dromedaries would appear suddenly, ravage, then disappear with their booty. They were the elusive inhabitants of the desert— the Bedouin—in the local idiom translated as *Badawi* from which the name Bedouin is derived.

The original Bedouins came from Oriental Asia and they brought the

At the time of the great pilgrimage, the holy city of Mecca cannot accommodate all the pilgrims, most of whom have to camp outside its walls. The crowded tents become a temporary city, sometimes with a population of over a million pilgrims.

camel with them into Arabia. It was the camel that made possible their survival in the arid Nefud and, finally, enabled them to reach the Hejaz.

Today, half or more of the people of Saudi Arabia live in oases, where they till the soil. The remainder are still nomadic, or villagers who are employed in the oil industry, in government work, in crafts, or in commerce. Towns have grown and there has been a great influx of workers from surrounding countries. But many of the Bedouins continue to lead the nomadic life they have led for many centuries. They move around the country, their journeys largely dictated by the distribution of water. Their wanderings are not aimless but follow a pattern that takes them to waterholes and rain-filled wells and pastures for their camels and other stock.

The ship of the desert

The camel is the mainstay of the nomad's life. In the desert of Rub'al Khali the Bedouins live mainly on camel milk for months at a time. The water from the holes is often too brackish for human beings but the camels drink it readily and thrive on it. In addition to being a source of all food, the camel provides the Bedouin with shelter and clothing, and gives him the mobility upon which his nomadic life depends.

A dromedary carrying a load of 330 pounds can travel at a steady two and a half miles per hour and cover thirty-one miles in twelve hours. This may not seem a great distance, but it has to be remembered that the camels are travelling over hot sand where there are no roads. A great deal depends on the age and strength of the camel. Some

of them can carry loads of 550 pounds.

The camel is noted for its ability to survive for long periods without drinking. The hardiest races of Arabian riding camels can go without water for periods of five to twelve days, but the ability to endure thirst varies according to the type of camel, the region in which it lives, and above all according to the season. In extremely dry conditions the camel requires water much more frequently than when the air is humid. Camels of the Sudan and Somalia can go without water for longer periods than the camels of Asia.

The ability to do without water seems to decrease eastwards and is least in camels on the high plains of Central Asia. Here, in the months of March and April, the animals cannot do without water for more than three days. Arabian riding camels, on the other hand, can go without water for twenty-five days in winter and five days in summer. By contrast, the Bactrian or Two-humped camel, can go for only forty-eight hours without water in hot weather.

When the camel drinks it takes in a great deal of water, but its ability to do without water for long periods does not arise from any special adaptation of the stomach. The water that the camel drinks remains in its stomach for only a short time. The secret lies in the hump and its store of fat.

Metabolic water

A hump containing sixty-six pounds of fat will release seventy pints of water. Albumens and fats burned chemically in any organism release water. From three and a half ounces of albumen about one and a half ounces of water are released. From

Two pilgrims to Mecca — a woman and child from a nomadic tribe of Khorosan in Northern Iran. Pilgrims like these come from all parts of the world to the holy city of Mecca. The world population of Moslems is now thought to number 500,000,000.

three and a half ounces of fat over three and a half ounces of water are produced. This is done by body chemistry. Hydrogen is released as a by-product of fat when it breaks down. Oxygen breathed in by a camel combines with the hydrogen to produce water. This water, known as metabolic water (that is water produced by the bodily functions of the animal itself), plus the moisture derived from the camel's other tissues, can keep it going normally for many days, even when it is carrying a load.

In addition, the camel loses only a little water by cooling. It sweats little, passes only small quantities of urine, and does not breathe rapidly. As a result of all this it may lose one-quarter of its body weight and suffer an increase in blood temperature without becoming seriously upset. It replaces the water by drinking. Once it is on a good diet it replaces the fat in its

hump which gradually swells to its former size.

Like other desert animals and certain animals from more northerly latitudes, the camel can go for months without drinking at all if it is eating wet food or green vegetation. But when the vegetation becomes scant and dry, as during the desert summer, the camel must have water because its food contains hardly any. It is then that its ability to do without is put to the test.

The Arabian camel has other adaptations for its desert life. It can close its nostrils completely to keep out the sand and has interlocking eyelashes to protect its eyes from the sun.

The camel replaces its water losses in one long draught and has been known to drink fifteen gallons at one time. It is this ability that enables it to make long journeys across the desert country where there are few wells. In addition, the

The present recalls the past—Arab horsemen of today galloping across the desert. It was horsemen like these who in the seventh century rode out from the deserts on the great mission of conquest that carried them to North Africa and the Orient.

The Arabian influence can be seen today even in the remote countries of Central Africa. The attire, weapons, and habits of these men of the Lamido of Maroua in Cameroon are identical to those of many centuries ago.

Bedouin. They are well known for their stoicism and for their acceptance of the harsh realities of their desert life. Even death is accepted with fatalistic calm. The customs of the nomadic Bedouin are quite different from those of the city dwellers. A Bedouin tent in the desert is furnished with mats, pillows, and containers for provisions and clothing. The men wear white tunics open at the neck and tied at the waist with a belt, and an embroidered jacket and cape. Their trousers are full at the hips and tight at the ankles. The typical headgear is a rectangular piece of cloth, held in place with a band of coloured rope, made of silk or camel hair.

The Bedouin women dress in red and blue and many of them are tattooed. They use make-up on their cheeks, forehead, and fingers. This make-up is produced from the crimson roots of a local bush known as Kahil, and the bright red fruits of a bush called 'Abal.

In his traditional songs the Bedouin sings proudly: "How many desert plateaux have I crossed. I have conquered them all from beginning to end". He lives hard, defends himself against aggressors with great courage and tenacity, spending long hours riding on a camel at speed across the desert. In the evenings he sits by the open fire, under an expansive sky that seems like a roof over the desert. He likes to spin tales and to listen to stories rich in poetic imagery. The Bedouin men were once famous for their raiding but this has been largely brought under control by modern governments.

The Bedouin cannot understand how people can live in towns and spend all their lives in one place, toiling day after day to do so. They are the gipsies of the desert, untramelled, free, and proud, and lead

camel is able to thrive on plants that are almost totally rejected by other grazing animals.

Besides supplying the Bedouin with milk, wool, and hides, the camel is useful in other ways. Its dung, compressed, is used for building shelters. It is also used as fuel. The camel is therefore an important animal in almost every way. So, the breeding of camels is important business among the Bedouin, and their sale a source of income. The Ship of the Desert may not be a thing of beauty but the lives of millions of desert people depend on it.

The Bedouin

Many writers have remarked on the dignity and nobility of the

Top:
Horsemen of Lamido
assemble to the call of
a silver trumpet, which
is the custom in the
desert. The weapons
raised to the sky sym-
bolize challenge and
battle.

Bottom left:
Horsemen of Lamido.

Bottom right: A horse-
man of Lamido.

A caravan arrives at an oasis in the Arabian desert.

Cultivation on the fringe of an oasis.

their hard nomadic lives by choice.

The Fellahin

The fellahin, or agricultural workers of the Egyptian, Syrian, and Arabian countryside, live in dwellings of stone and packed earth. Each home has a flat roof where the family sleeps on the hottest nights and where they put out their harvest to dry. Each dwelling is quadrangular in shape and divided into two rooms. The fireplace and stable for the animals are on one side of the division; the household bedding and food supplies are on the other.

Depending on the area in which they live, the fellahin cultivate wheat, millet, barley, maize, vegetables, figs, almonds, and dates. The harvests in the poorest areas are meagre and in most places equipment and methods are out of date. For example, the ploughshares are made of wood and the threshing machines consist of long boards studded with nails or sharp stones.

In spite of their extreme poverty, the fellahin were once continually raided by the Bedouin. The rich merchants, safe inside the city walls, were free from such raids; but the peasants outside were easily overcome by the raiders who sacked the harvest and stole women and children. To this day, the fellahin of the Nefud and the Hejaz deserts are resigned to paying tribute to the Bedouin in order to be left in peace.

Black gold

All deserts being basically alike—

34

great heat, low rainfall, scarcity of water, and resulting lack of vegetation—life in the deserts of Arabia, for both nomads and settlers, is on the whole typical of life in other deserts. There are local differences but in all the deserts of the Middle East the way of life is very similar.

The deserts of Arabia are rich in one great natural resource—the black gold beneath the red sands—oil. This resource brings great wealth to the countries that possess it. Yet even today the wealth is far from fairly distributed among the citizens of the producing countries. One section of the community enjoys fabulous fortune, while the other and much larger group still lives in abject poverty. The ancient castles of the caliphs have been replaced by the modern villas of the oil princes—buildings surrounded by reservoirs and swimming pools, woodlands, fragrant gardens and, not far distant, runways for private jet aircraft. But the fellahin still live in their huts of earth and stone.

In the Arabian desert, as in others in the Middle East, oil pipelines stretch endlessly across the sands. It has been estimated that one-third of the world's oil lies hidden in this region. Certainly there are sufficient quantities there to furnish all the oil requirements of Europe.

The first discovery of oil in the desert was made by the Australian William D'Arcy, early this century. Drilling for oil first began in Southern Iran. Discovery of other oil wells proceeded apace and drillings became more and more numerous. After World War I oil was being pumped in Iraq. In the 1930s the search for oil began in Saudi Arabia. After World War II, Kuwait, the Sultanate of Muscat, and the Sheikdoms of the Coast of Pirates became oil producing countries. The British, the Americans, and now the French and Italians operate the wells in association with the local governments. The search for oil goes on in the Persian Gulf where the oil fields and their associated

A drilling machine at work in the sands of the Kuwait desert in the Arabian Peninsula. Beneath the sands of Kuwait lies one of the richest oil fields in the world.

Drilling for oil in the desert of Iraq.

geological formations extend far under the sea.

The search for new oil-fields goes on all the time, with geologists playing the leading role, as they are the professional readers of Nature's signs. No drilling begins without a favourable report from the geologist in the field.

The most important member of any surveying party is a Bedouin who is famed for his skill in desert tracking. The party will use radios and compasses to help them find

The camp of a geological survey party in the Arabian desert during field operations.

their way, but the Bedouin guide carries in his head much of the knowledge that will keep the party on course and prevent it from becoming lost.

True Bedouins have highly developed powers of observation. As they go along, they take note of every change in the plant life or the characteristics of the sand dunes. Their sense of direction is extremely acute. They can find their way by taking note of the position of the sun and making allowances for variations at different times of the day and year.

The Bedouin is also an expert tracker able to read the signs left by animals and their comings and goings. He also uses his nose a great deal to sniff the breeze.

Saved in the New World

The Arabian oryx is a large antelope now almost extinct on its home range. Uncontrolled hunting by the Bedouin, and latterly by wealthy hunters using fast cars, has been responsible for this catastrophic decline and it became obvious that the oryx was heading for total extinction if no effort was made to save it. The Fauna Preservation Society of Great Britain made the effort in 1962. An expedition led by Major Grimwood and financed by the World Wildlife Fund and other bodies succeeded in capturing three specimens. These animals were sent to a desert reserve in Phoenix, Arizona, along with one contributed by the London Zoo, one by

An oil pumping station at Haft Kel in the Iranian desert. The oil that flows through the pipelines is the life blood of many desert countries today.

37

Villagers outside a Qala in the desert of Khorosan in Iran.

the Ruler of Kuwait, and four by King Ibn-Saud, to form a breeding stock.

This venture has proved successful. Five Arabian oryxes were born in the two captive herds in the United States between December 1967 and April 1968. Two were born at Phoenix Zoo, Arizona, one of which died thirty-six hours later. A male was born at Los Angeles Zoo in February, a male at Phoenix in March, and another female at Phoenix on April 26th. If the present figure of 11 oryxes still existing in Arabia is correct, then the present-day United States population of Arabian oryxes is higher than that in the animal's native land.

The reptiles

Some lizards of the Arabian desert are used as food by the Bedouin. One species, the dabb, is twenty-eight inches long and has a thick, spiny tail which it lashes about to defend itself. Adult dabbs feed on leaves and fruits but the young ones are insectivorous. During the heat of the day the dabb lies up in rock shelters or digs itself down into the sand. The dabb is found in Egypt east of the Nile and in Sinai as well as Arabia.

Another common lizard of the Empty Quarter is the Hungarian Skink which is about four inches long. These lizards literally swim just under the surface of the sand. The Bedouin children are adept at catching them.

Destruction of wildlife

On a journey across the desert today one can still see a variety of snakes, and birds like eagles, hawks, falcons, sand grouse, vultures, owls and ravens. But gazelles, once so common, are becoming rare through overhunting, and the traveller is not likely to see one speeding across the sandy plain. The herds of hundreds are a thing of the past and today the Saudi Arabian government is trying to save the remnants. The sorry tale of the destruction of Arabian wildlife began with the introduction of modern firearms and was expedited by the motor car. Oil made the sheiks wealthy and they could afford both, so it became a common sight to see antelope hunted by men in fast cars and using machine guns. Poaching sheiks from the north still behave in this way.

It was this type of hunting that almost killed off the oryx; and the remainder will go unless it is forbidden. In the old days the man who could track down and kill an oryx was a hunter who was respected and it was indeed a considerable accomplishment. But to run an animal to the point of collapse and then shoot it is something else entirely.

Jordan now protects gazelles by law and has 1,500 square miles National Park in which all wildlife is protected. King Hussein took this step after he received the reports of the two Mountfort expeditions. The remaining gazelles of Jordan are still under threat from wealthy poachers from neighbouring states. The local Bedouin catch calves and sell them into captivity but are not responsible for the threatened extinction of the species. This threat comes from the motorist hunter with his sub machine-gun.

Iran eastwards

Between Dasht-I-Kavir and Dasht-I-Lut, two of the great deserts of Iran, there is a large area of sand and steppe dotted with oases and villages. Here we find the usual dualism of the desert areas of the Middle East—nomads and settlers. But the villages in this area have an interest of their own. They are fortified villages known as Qala.

These Qala, of which there are thousands in an area about the size of Britain, are the products of a long, unsettled history. This part of the world was subject to continuous

In the Shirvan region of the Khorosan desert. The scant herbage provides grazing for herds of domestic livestock. Sheep and goats have been responsible over the centuries for the creation of desert by overgrazing.

invasion, the most terrible of which was that of the Mongols under Genghis Khan in the thirteenth century. The people reacted to such threats by fortifying their settlements. So the Qala came into being as a defence against raiders — whether local tribesmen, Turks, or invading Mongols. The Qala was the most successful attempt made by any desert people to create a defensive system against hostile forces.

But the Qala is more than a fortified village. Its sturdy walls protect the people of the villages against dust and wind. In this area the sky is hidden during the entire day by a haze. This is caused by dust which is raised by the wind during the hottest hours. From June until September, the wind blows from the desert of Kara-Kum in Russia. This is "the wind of the one hundred and twenty days." The Qala protects the village people against it as against invaders.

A Qala has mud walls with battlements and sentry towers.

The moles of the desert

This terracotta statuette representing a working camel, was sculpted by an unknown village artist in Afghanistan.

In their constant battle to ensure their water supply the desert peoples of the Middle East developed a system known as the Quanat, or foggara. This is a sloping tunnel leading from the village, or storage place near it, to an underground source of water. The water flows along the Quanat in a steady trickle. Several Quanats may tap a source of water at different points and converge on the village, thus increasing the supply. They are usually several miles long; some carry water for twenty-five to thirty miles.

A Quanat is really like a mole tunnel except that it slopes from beginning to end to allow the water to run. Even in its construction the men who excavate the tunnel work like moles. They burrow under the desert, working in darkness or semi-darkness and, like moles, the material they excavate is sent to the surface via shafts that are dug at intervals of thirty to fifty yards. One man, the burrower, extends the tunnel, testing the incline by means of a length of string along which a drop of water is made to run. He is not aiming at level digging, the incline must be maintained and the string with its bead of water acts as a spirit level.

The material excavated by the burrower is collected by another man who carries it to the base of a shaft in a bag that holds about sixty pounds. This bag is raised to the surface by another man operating a windlass. Boys work in the narrower Quanats which are too small for a man. Driving a Quanat can be very dangerous work because the roof might fall in. Tunnels are therefore made as narrow as possible and form a triangle at the top as a safety measure.

The piles of dirt brought to the surface and dumped around the mouth of the shaft look like large doughnuts when viewed from the air. Such rings mark the course of the tunnel from the water source to the village on lower ground. Trees grow round the basin at the terminal, a symbol of yet another victory over the desert.

There are thousands of Quanats in Iran, Arabia, Afghanistan and the Sahara, many of them unfinished. The work is never ending. New tunnels are excavated and old ones repaired. Many begun genera-

A camel caravan makes its way across the bare, hostile terrain of Kabul in Afghanistan.

*A caravan of nomads
with their camels leaving
the Khyber Pass in search
of fresh pasture for their animals.*

tions ago are still not finished. The digging of Quanats is a specialized trade and sometimes a family business. It is also dangerous work and the tunnels have claimed many victims, buried while digging.

The vertical desert

Afghanistan is a mountainous country of high plateaux and deep valleys without an outlet to the sea. It is bounded by high mountain ranges like the Hindu Kush, reaching 24,000 feet, and others ranging from 8,000 feet to over 15,000 feet.

Country like this may not present the usual image of a desert. There are no great flat expanses reaching to the horizon. The plains are few, but the gigantic mountains have been denuded by erosion. The nature of the land is therefore desert and because of the steepness of the terrain Afghanistan is sometimes described as a vertical desert.

The nomadic population of Afghanistan is large and each tribe has traditions that have been handed down for thousands of years. These nomads raise sheep and goats, use camels as beasts of burden, and live in black tents made from animal skins sewn together.

In spring and summer the Afghan nomads travel to the highest pastures with their stock, even beyond the 6,000 to 9,000 feet mark. Many of them are from Pakistan; they come through the Khyber Pass and other routes in summer to seek fresh pastures high in Afghanistan.

All these people travel slowly at the grazing pace of their livestock, which means that they do not cover more than ten miles a day. Their migration continues through spring and summer and in winter they

An Afghan woman weaving a carpet.

The leader of a caravan takes a rest during the long journey across the Central Highlands of Afghanistan, in the region of Jalalabad.

move down to the low ground where there is no snow. Like the nomads of other deserts, they are hardy people and great traditionalists.

Now that the hectic days of raids and guerilla warfare are over, these nomads expend their energy and test their skill and ability in sport. One of their traditional sports is Buz-Kasci, which means literally "grab the goat". Opposing groups of tribesmen, daring horsemen mounted on swift, specially trained horses, line up at opposing goalposts. Between them stands the goat. Each horseman of each team must succeed, by any means at all and without dismounting from his horse, in grabbing the goat and forcing his way through to the opposite goalpost. In this he has the support of his own side who help him in any way they can to force a way through the opposing wall of horsemen. The opposition in their turn have to try to take the goat away from the opponent and prevent him reaching their goal. The game is played for a prescribed length of time and the team that carries the goat to the opposite goal most often is the winner.

This is Rugby with players on horseback and a goat as a ball.

CHAPTER 4

THE DESERTS
OF ASIA

As one travels inland in Asia the air becomes steadily drier and the rainfall decreases. The steppes or semi arid regions give way to prairie, then to semi-desert, and finally to desert. It was through this great central belt, the Steppes Corridor, that Genghis Khan and Marco Polo travelled long ago, and for centuries it was the great trade route between the Mediterranean world and China. The vastness of this great hinterland is almost incomprehensible to those who have not crossed it and its dryness is due to its long distance from the sea.

The entire northern border of India is protected from nomadic invaders by a great mountain range about five miles high, and the only way to reach India by land from the north is through the narrow mountain passes. The most famous of these is the Khyber Pass, a gateway for trade and the historic route of invaders from the deserts on the other side of the Himalayas.

The nomads who live in this area today face the same problems of survival, and live much the same lives as their ancestors in these arid barren lands. They are wandering tribesman who swarm through the Khyber Pass in the Hindu Kush to the plateau of Iran and northwards into Soviet Middle Asia. They have no regard for national boundaries. Their movements are concerned entirely with survival. They wrest a living from grudging semi-desert land by constant travel with their animals to new grazing areas. Their migrations are south in autumn and north in spring.

The Great Desert of India has the lowest population density in the entire country. The desert region called the Thar is partly in India and partly in Pakistan. A large part of the Indian province of Rajasthan, which is desert, lies in the eastern part of the Thar, but its aridity is tempered by steppes that reach down to the waters of the Chambal river. Farther south in Pakistan the desert becomes the Sind. The people of all these areas live mainly in villages close to springs.

Between the totally arid region of the Thar, and the steppe area of Rajasthan, rise the peaks of the Aravalli hills. On one of these hills, at the height of 5,100 feet, is the Peak of Wisdom, a sacred rock called Mount Apu, which, according to local legend, is the birthplace of the warlike race of *Rajput*.

Creation by fire

The people of Rajput, who live in the desert of Rajasthan today, believe completely in the story of their creation. The story is that the Hindu god, Vishnu, decided to create a race of men strong and

The famous Khyber Pass, linking the deserts of Afghanistan and Pakistan—the historic route for invaders entering India.

A wooden image representing the founder of the Chauhan family in the Thar desert. This is a common type of wood carving.

An Indian village beside an oasis in the Thar desert, State of Rajasthan.

courageous enough to survive in the desert and to overcome any invading enemy. On Mount Apu he lit a sacred fire and from its flames the race of Rajput was born. The people who live in the area today believe they are the descendants of the first families created by this fire.

Another part of the Rajput story tells how the first woman was created. It does not differ widely from that of the creation in Genesis. After Vishnu had created man he decided to give him a companion, but he found that he had used up all the solid material so he had to fashion woman as best he could and in the end he made her a composite—giving her characteristics and features of things he had already created: the roundness of the moon, the curves of the ramblers, the clinging of the vines, the quivering of the grass, the slenderness of the reeds, the lightness of the leaves, the eye of the desert gazelle and the fickleness and violence of the desert winds. To these he added the shyness of the desert hare, the vanity of the peacock, the hardness of the diamond, the softness of the parrot's stomach feathers, the sweetness of honey, the cruelty of the tiger and the heat of fire. He blended them all together into woman and gave her to man as a companion.

The Rajput of India can be compared to the Knights of the Round Table, for they were noble warriors in the service of Indian kings and princes. Sometimes the kings and princes themselves were Rajputs.

To visit the land of the Rajput the traveller has to cross seemingly limitless stretches of sand. The wise traveller will leave each day at the first light of dawn so that he can make good progress before the heat of the day begins. Along the route he will pass through places steeped in Rajput history and the history of the Indian Middle Ages. Such places played an important role in the battles against invaders; they were strong points in the defence of the fertile and cultivated regions.

Lost cities and Jai kings

The Desert of the Thar with its desolate sentinel mountains was the stage on which the daring Rajputs played out their warlike drama over the centuries. One such place is the city of Amber, the ancient capital of Rajasthan. The walls of Amber still stand, rising from the sands and rocks of the valley. But it is a deserted city, silent and dead in the milk-white heat of the day, a monument to the Rajput dynasty that ruled it for centuries until 1728.

Within Amber's protecting walls is the Palace of the Jai kings, who fought off the invading Moguls and repelled them by force of arms, although they later joined them as allies.

A few miles from Amber is the city of Jaipur, an anthill of activity compared with the deserted and silent Amber. Jaipur, the new capital city of Rajasthan, was designed by King Jai Singh II in 1728 after he had abandoned Amber. It was designed as a citadel against the desert—a defence against the forces

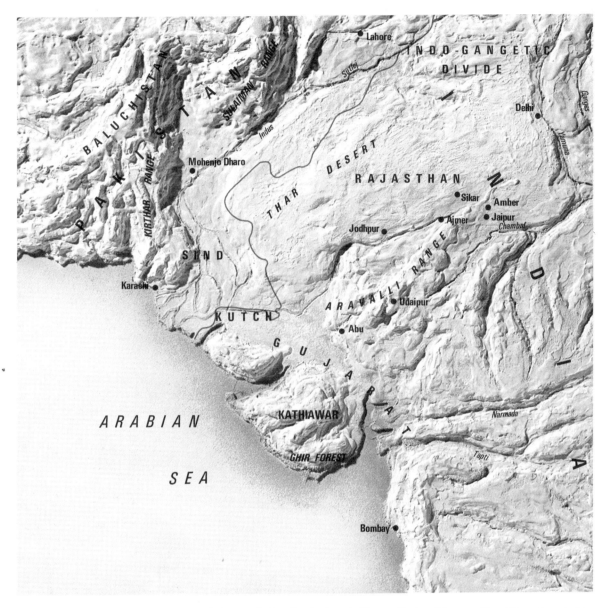

of nature. Its streets are straight and so planned that they act as a barrier against the wind and dust of the desert. The houses, from the humblest dwellings of the poor to the famous Palace of the Wind that the king built for himself and his court, are designed to keep out the heat and remain cool inside.

The Palace of the Wind was constructed of native stone—the pink stone of the Thar desert. It has thousands of small windows and verandas and is always cool because of the free circulation of air. Thus Jaipur has its defence against heat, wind, and dust. It has no strategic defences of any kind, no prepared positions and no fortresses. The bravery of the Rajput warriors within its walls, and in the castles of Amber, were always considered sufficient to protect the valley from invasion by enemies.

In the streets of Jaipur today the city people mingle with those from the caravans and elsewhere and there are few, if any, of the Rajput

The Thar desert between India and Pakistan is almost entirely of sand. The desert of Sind, to the west, is mostly flat alluvial country, the country of the Indus, where one of the greatest civilizations of the ancient world flourished 3,000 years B.C.

warriors living there. The desert saved them and in the desert they still live, proud of their history and preserving their ways. It is in the desert that one finds the living descendants of the ancient Rajputs and the monuments that have survived the centuries.

Massacre at Kathiawar

If you travel in the land of the Rajput you will see a desert of monotonous rocky ridges tapering off to the horizon. Then suddenly on the spine of one of these ridges you will come across monuments like tombstones standing out against the sky. Some still remain upright, others lean over, yet others have crashed to the ground. Some have been chiselled and burned by the sun. Many lie broken and crumbling. On each stone the figure of a knight has been carved with primitive skill.

These monuments commemorate the massacre of over one hundred Rajput Knight Errants. The warriors were ambushed and

A sand storm in the Thar desert in Rajasthan. Storms like this bring all movement to a halt. Men and animals have to take what shelter they can and sit out the storm.

Thar nomads and their camels leaving the ancient fortified city of Amber, once a metropolis of the great Indus civilization.

slaughtered when they were hastening to the defence of a castle belonging to one of the princes of Kathiawar. They fought for many days on the heights before they were overwhelmed. All of them perished. Years later, their friend the prince remembered them and erected a pillar to each of them bearing the warrior's effigy, name, and a written account of his most courageous deeds.

Today a lonely shepherd stands guard over these monuments to long dead warriors. The grandparents of the shepherd's grandparents were Rajput warriors and he keeps vigil over the memorials to the dead. On his face is the intense look and all the fierceness of the Rajput warriors of long ago.

The Indus civilization

Beyond the sands of the Thar and the land of the Rajput warriors lie the ruins of the great civilization of the Indus—one of the highest civilizations of the ancient past. The ruins lie in the Pakistan area of the Indo-Pakistan desert. From a plane the Indus River appears as a shiny ribbon flowing through the desert and often sand and water meet without a shadow of greenery to mark their boundary.

For many centuries the Indus has been flowing through desert lands that were once green. Soon it is hoped the desert will become green again and more populated, for here in Pakistan the Sind is being transformed by a gigantic irrigation project.

It is well known that the civilization that once flowered in the Sind was made possible by a network of irrigation canals that made the land productive. The inhabitants of the Sind were able to live because they had water. The countryside encircled two villages with its lush greenery. As the irrigation canal spread out, the produce from the land increased and the old cities of Harappa and Mohenjo Dharo became great metropolises.

Harappa and Mohenjo Dharo were the pivot of the most ancient civilization of India and the highest civilization of prehistoric times. The ruins of the city of Harappa were discovered by accident. In 1856, when India belonged to Britain, the Viceroy granted a lease to two brothers, John and William Brunton, to build a railway across the desert from Karachi to Lahore.

A solitary shepherd keeps watch over his flocks near an oasis on the edge of the Thar desert.

Jaipur is the largest capital in the State of Rajasthan. The buildings are of rose stone from the Thar desert. The Palace of the Wind in the centre of the city was built in the first half of the eighth century.

During the construction, the brothers discovered in the sand a gigantic storage place, made of terracotta bricks. They utilized this place as a cave and the bricks for building up the embankment.

Many years later it was discovered that for a distance of almost 125 miles the railway line ran over an embankment of bricks dating from the Third Millenium before Christ. These ancient bricks being used in constructing a nineteenth-century railway had been part of the old irrigation system of Harappa thousands of years before.

The desert takes over

The Indus civilization still represents one of the greatest archaeological and cultural enigmas in history and there is no answer to the question of how it came to an end.

It is likely that various factors contributed. The desert was most likely one of them. After thousands of years of expansion, the vital force reached a crisis. The desert was always there, right on the threshold of the irrigated regions and always ready to creep back

These sculptured tombstones tell the story of the Rajput horsemen massacred in an ambush on the outskirts of Kathiawar. This is hallowed ground still tended by a shepherd whose great grandparents were Rajput warriors.

Two of the Kathiawar tombstones showing carvings of Rajput horsemen who were killed in the massacre.

jab region, there is a triangular tract of land of nearly five million acres. The base of this triangle runs for about 65 miles along the salt range to the north and stretches for about 175 miles to its apex in the south. In the old days the Indus river flowed through the middle of this area, depositing huge quantities of sand and silt. In the view of some researchers the river changed its course to the west, thus changing the landscape. The sand dunes here arise from fine material blown from the coastal and desert regions of Sind and Rajasthan. The plant life is mostly low brush and scanty grass on which camels browse. Archaeologists have found no evidence of early occupation such as the civilizations of Harappa and Mohenjo Dharo, but they have discovered evidence of population about the 14th century.

The area is now being rapidly developed. Small towns and villages are being built and industries have been introduced and are growing—sugar refineries, cotton and woollen mills, and a cement factory. There are hundreds of villages, each with forty or fifty houses, occupying about a hundred acres. Round each village there is a belt of green and alongside there are fifty acres of timber. Each settler is permitted to work fifteen acres of land not more than a mile and a half from his village. These he must cultivate satisfactorily in order to retain them.

In certain areas masonry wells have been used for years to supply water for small areas. Although irrigation canals supply the large regions, wells can provide a simpler solution to the water problem in small areas. It is hoped that by using a system of tubes each well will be able to supply water to irrigate up to 150 acres.

again if man relaxed his grip. Possibly the people of Harappa and Mohenjo Dharo began to neglect the upkeep of their irrigation canals, thus allowing the sand to close in. The river, no longer controlled, would flood the ports. No one really knows but this seems the most likely chain of events. Decadence would then quickly set in, culminating in the destruction and total abandonment of the area.

The final blow came when hordes of warriors swept across the desert from the north and ground the great civilization of the Indus under their horses' hoofs. Until then the horse had been unknown in these parts. Horse and warrior, along with the forces of the desert, brought about the end of the civilization of the desert. Excavations at Mohenjo Dharo and Harappa have brought to light the skeletons of the last defenders who were massacred, weapons in hand. The skeletons of the women and children who died with them have also been found.

Modern development

In Western Pakistan, in the Pun-

Salt water

One of the great problems in this region is salty water. When rain falls on land it is free from salt but it takes up soluble salts in the soil as it runs over the ground. When it drains downwards it carries away a certain amount of salt from the surface. Where rainfall is low, however, salt accumulates from irrigation waters. If there is not a proper balance between the amount of salt being spread by irrigation waters and the amount being carried away in solution by drainage water, plants cannot grow. This problem is receiving much study and the United Nations Food and Agricultural Organization is presently working on it in an attempt to solve it in the Indus valley.

It has been estimated that the first half mile of the earth's crust contains about ten million cubic miles of water. According to the UNESCO *Courier* it would take the annual flow of all the earth's rivers 132 years to fill such a reservoir. So there is no scarcity of water under the earth. The problem is to make use of it on the surface.

Some day desert peoples will find better ways of using ground water. All the great civilizations of the ancient East have evolved in desert regions where people had very little water and had to make the best use

Fishermen with their nets on the banks of the Indus river which flows through the sands of the Sind desert.

An unknown artist of the Sind desert made this carving in wood. It shows the face and headgear of a caravan leader.

The ancient invaders of the Occidental/Indian desert brought the hitherto unknown horse to that part of the continent. The horse is here colourfully depicted in cloth and wool.

of what little they had. A. J. Toynbee has said that the greater the ease of the environment the weaker the stimulus towards civilization. The reverse of this is that the tougher the environment the greater the stimulus. This certainly seems to have applied to life in the desert long ago. If man today would use his scientific and technological knowledge, and his wealth, in perfecting methods used years ago in the deserts, many water supply problems would be quickly overcome and much desert land could be brought into production.

Water tunnels

The pipelines discussed in the last chapter, which carry water underground, are sometimes referred to as galleries. They are found in many countries and are called by many different names such as Kanats, Quanats and Ghanats. But all perform the same service. They tap pockets of underground water at the bottom of mountains and carry it through underground tunnels for many miles to areas where crops can be grown. It is estimated that there are 30,000 tunnels in Iran and 300,000 miles of underground tunnels between North West Africa and the eastern perimeter of Central Asia. In many communities large and small, the only available water comes from such underground tunnels.

Extensive networks of kanat tunnels exist in places where there is nothing on the surface to betray the presence of underground water and provide an illustration of the ingenuity of desert peoples. The kanat, combined with drilled wells, could still be used to increase water supply in areas where electricity is too scarce to be used in pumping it.

Modern man uses new tools to find water in the desert. One method used for finding underground water is a variation of the radio prospecting techniques used in locating minerals. Radio waves are reflected from the surface of the underground water and are picked up by an aeroplane flying overhead. By using this method engineers can find concentrations of underground water and can even tell how salty it is by the angle of reflection, which varies according to salinity. It may well be that underneath the desert sands there are greater underground reservoirs of fresh and mineralized waters than anyone has realized. As scientists learn more about the structure of the earth beneath the desert, local water resources may become available for use on the surface.

Tree planting

The Pakistani government authorities have planted fourteen million trees in the past ten years as part of a gigantic plan to reclaim all the lands lost to the desert sand during thousands of years. And this is only the first step in a gigantic plan. The struggle against the encroachment of the desert, and the attempt to restore existing desert to productive land, is intimately bound up with the attempt to bring back vegetation. Trees are important units in the battle. The battle for water and fertility is also a battle for vegetation. The transformation of the desert will depend on the planting, wherever possible, of trees and more trees so that a green carpet will gradually unroll to cover the old red carpet of the desert.

The story of the desert from the days of Harappa and Mohenjo Dharo is a story of progression, but not always one of progress. First of all people change the desert land into one where plants and trees can grow. The red of the desert becomes green with vegetation. The plants that grow in the area then help by adding moisture to the air that can fall back again as rain. When agriculture is abandoned the vegetation disappears and the rain ceases. The land dries up, the wind becomes the master, and the topsoil is blown about. Gradually, over the centuries, rocks and soil are pulverized into sand. But the process is being reversed again today. In places where water is being fed into irrigation canals the desert is being tamed once more.

Much the same cycle of events has taken place in other desert areas. The Negeve in Israel was a vast, harsh expanse of barren ground for thousands of years before the present-day Israelis began to work on it to make it productive. But it had been tamed once before by ancient people known as the Nabateans who, with great ingenuity, had constructed small underground cisterns.

Reclamation

Many great water conservation schemes and irrigation schemes are operating in the world today. The Soviet government is taming the Don, the Volga, the Amu Darya and other great river systems to increase production on 70,000,000 arid acres. Turkey completed a great irrigation scheme in 1949. In Iraq the United Nations Food and Agricultural Organization sent in a British engineer, John Ramsay, to teach the people there how to dig wells using modern equipment and techniques. Before he arrived the nomadic tribes depended on 180 scattered shallow wells to water themselves and their animals. With-

in six years, 270 deep wells had been sunk in the desert, changing the whole outlook for the nomadic peoples. Where they had gone short of water and food and fought for both, they now had ample for all. The green acres increased in number and mortality fell among men and beasts.

But many problems arising from irrigation still remain. Water carries salts in solution and if allowed to lie in one place it evaporates and leaves the salt behind. In addition it brings up salts already partly leached into the ground. Irrigation schemes, to be successful, must arrange for overflow and drainage. Building dams brings problems because of silting up over the years. Watersheds have to be carefully managed because if they are denuded of trees the rivers dry up.

Forest of Ghir

One of the strangest sights of the

A green spot in the Indian desert. Here the nomads find water, and grazing for their animals, and can settle for a short period. Small-scale irrigation can make life possible in such lonely spots in the desert.

Workers prepare clay bricks in a desert village. The bricks are then baked hard in the sun.

Inhabitants of a village in the Sind desert. One of the women is wearing a special face covering as a protection against windblown sand.

Indo-Pakistan Desert is the Forest of Ghir, the only example in the world of an extensive forest in a desert. But it is not a forest in the ordinary sense, for it is neither green nor damp, nor cool with shadows. No leafy undergrowth covers the earth. The Ghir is an inferno of heat. The earth is red-brown dust. The trees are giant shrubs, leafless but bristling with thorns and with trunks contorted and entwined. Everything is hot and the colour of burnt sienna—earth and tree stumps and thorns, and the faces and clothing of anyone who enters there.

There are lions in the Forest of Ghir—the last left in the whole of Asia. The Ghir is their last refuge and they number about 80, which is a fraction of the original population. The lions now have a restricted distribution in the Ghir and live in peaceful coexistence with the nomadic people there. They prey upon the gazelles and other animals of

the forest and are never a threat to people passing through, even when the travellers are on foot and at close range. Lions and people of the Ghir are covered, like the trees, with red dust.

Lions of the Ghir

Alexander the Great hunted the lions of the Ghir when he invaded India and there are a few miniatures in existence depicting the great king on horseback, armed with his short, lethal spear, hunting these Indian lions. It is commonly believed that there are no lions in India, which, as we have just seen, is not true. But if the few remaining lions in the Ghir are allowed to disappear it will become true.

The present author visited the Ghir recently to film the lions. After many hours of travelling by car and jeep the party had a long march on foot, in heat and dust, to reach the forest. Suddenly the lions were standing right before us covered, as were the filming party, with reddish-brown dust. They were panting from the suffocating heat. Men and beasts stopped a few steps away from each other, unable to move. The lions stared, their mouths half open showing their teeth, and looked anything but reassuring. In reality the lions of the Ghir are not aggressive at all. Their mouth is half open like that because of the heat. The leader of the unit knew them well and everyone had faith in him, although standing unarmed a few yards away from a pride of lions is a strange sensation. At least in Africa one hunts and photographs lions from a jeep, but here on foot one feels helpless and vulnerable. Nevertheless, moving round and about the beasts film shots were taken, with increasing confidence and without

risk. Pictures of the lions were, moreover, shot with the aid of flash bulbs and the blinding flashes did not perturb the lions in the least.

There were five lions in the pride: a big male and a female with three cubs. The cubs were playing round their mother, clawing at her, trying to bite her tail with their teeth, and rolling over with their paws in the air. All of a sudden we had a surprise. From the thorn bushes behind the lioness appeared a group of women, nomadic peasants carrying heavy bundles of wood on their heads. The lioness, startled, looked at them and let out a deep, rumbling growl. We glanced swiftly at our leader, imagining that he would be reaching for his rifle. Then we looked at the women who we were sure would beat a hasty retreat, but nothing of the sort

happened. Our leader was lighting a cigarette and the women walked on almost brushing against the crouching lioness who did not trouble even to look at them. She had enough to do defending herself against her irrepressible cubs.

Questioning the leader later about this incident he answered: "When there were many of them these lions were dangerous, but now that they are so few they do not pose any problem. In these parts no one recalls a single case of a man being attacked by a lion."

Chant to the lions

The nomadic peasants in this region have a dance during which they chant to the lions of the Ghir. Above the rhythmic beating of the drums the chanting chorus ends:

The ruins of the city of Mohenjo Dharo in the Sind desert. This once great metropolis, an architectural monument to a bygone age, was one of the centres of the Indus civilization three thousand years before the birth of Christ. At that time the surrounding desert was fertile land producing crops. The surrounding desert is also also a monument—to man's misuse of his environment.

"Friend lion, fortunate king of
  this forest
  You sleep all day
While we till the soil, in the sun.
  Friend lion, at night you hunt
    with ease
That food which we extract from
    the earth with so much toil.
  Friend lion, fortunate king of
    this forest
Sleep peacefully all the rest of
    your days.
  You alone are strong enough
To endure the heat of Thar
  The heat of the desert that
    kills."

The fabulous Gobi

One of the most famous deserts
in the world is the Gobi. It is part
of the great Taklamakan Desert
which extends from Western China
to Mongolia. In a way it is all part
of a greater desert area extending
from the plains of India and the
Hindu Kush mountains to the Gobi
itself, the vast area known as the
Central Asian Desert. This desert
area stretches for more than 2,000
miles and the Gobi is the last great
obstacle to caravans on their way
to the lowlands of China and the
Pacific coast. The Gobi stretches
1,000 miles across Asia and is a
wasteland of salt basins and desolate scrub.

One of the great explorers who
crossed the Asian deserts was Marco
Polo. He was also the first European
to cross the wasteland of China and
bring back a detailed account of
what he saw. But one of the best
descriptions of the Gobi was written
by an explorer who crossed it in
1886. This young British army
officer, Francis Younghusband, described his experiences in a book
called *The Heart of a Continent*.

"No grass could be seen, and in
its place the country was covered
with dry and stunted plants, burned
brown by the sun by day and nipped
by the frost by night. Not a sound
could be heard and scarcely a living
thing seen as we plodded along
slowly but steadily over the seemingly interminable plains."

Younghusband and his group
travelled from three o'clock in the
afternoon until midnight each day
in order to escape the heat. They
used the stars as a means of navigation and they marked each one as it
disappeared below the horizon to
indicate the time of night. Younghusband goes on to describe a part
of his journey in the eastern end
of the Desert of Dzungaria:

"Nothing we have passed hitherto can compare with it—a succession of gravel ranges without any
sign of life, animal or vegetable, and

not a drop of water. We were gradually descending to a very low level. The sun was getting higher and higher, the wind hotter and hotter, until I shrank from it as from the blast of a furnace."

Roy Chapman Andrews

Crossing the deserts of Central Asia has been a challenge to the courage and ability of many explorers. One of the most famous of these was the American, Roy Chapman Andrews. In 1922 and the following years, Dr. Andrews led a number of scientific expeditions in Asia, sponsored by the American Museum of Natural History. These expeditions are famous because they led to the discovery of dinosaurs and their eggs, and other dinosaurs that are thought to have been predators on the eggs. The scientists discovered huge horned dinosaurs and the fossilized bones of reptile species that had already been found in America. This was an indication that the early ancestors of these animals had, like man himself, migrated from Asia to North America by way of an old land bridge. The sands of the Gobi, like the ice of Mongolia and Alaska, had preserved the dinosaurs' remains for millions of years.

The expeditions led by Dr. Andrews in the Gobi Desert were hazardous undertakings because of the waterless wastelands they had to cross. Petrol for motor cars had to be carried on the backs of animals, sometimes for distances of 800 miles. But in spite of the difficult conditions, these expeditions brought back some of the most exciting prehistoric treasures ever found.

There is an interesting sidelight on the Andrews' discoveries. In 1913, Roy Chapman Andrews was a guest at a Buddhist monastery located between Burma and China. The great American palaeontologist was at that time conducting research in Asia but had been unable to find the slightest trace of the evidence he was looking for. The Father Superior consoled the explorer who was embittered by the almost certain failure of his expedition, and exhorted him to visit the Gobi Desert in Mongolia.

"Down there," the Buddhist monk said, "you will find proof of the beginnings of mammal life."

Between 1919 and 1930, as a result of his adventurous explorations, Roy Chapman Andrews unearthed the Gobi's secrets—the eggs and entire skeletons of dinosaurs, and the skeleton of Baluchitherium, the largest mammal that ever lived. The holy man, it seems, had given the modern scientist a key. But how did this Buddhist monk, spending his life in prayer in a monastery 3,000 miles from the Gobi Desert, know about the remains of these ancient animals?

Roy Chapman Andrews discovered new geological forms and some of the richest fossil fields known to the world. Some of the oldest mammals were discovered, including the skull and other parts of Baluchitherium, the largest known land mammal. Research in this field went on in Central Asia until 1932 and Roy Chapman Andrews became director of the American Museum of Natural History from 1935 until he retired in 1942.

Other researchers followed Roy Chapman Andrews. In the years 1963 and 1965 an expedition of Polish and Mongolian scientists, under the direction of Professor Zofia Kielan-Jaworowska, unearthed eleven whole skeletons of dinosaurs, as well as nests con-

This piece of sculpture representing a man is by an unknown artist who lived 14,000 years ago in the Sind desert.

A Hindu hermit photographed near the outskirts of Daulatabad, Iran.

59

A lioness photographed in the forest of Ghir in the heart of the desolate area of Gujrat. The forest is covered in dry red dust. The twisted trees and the thorny shrubs are completely bare of leaves.

taining their eggs, and hundreds of mammal skulls perfectly preserved.

The Gobi desert has proved to be a natural conservation site of the remains of long extinct species. In any hot, dry, climate the chances of nature preserving such precious relics are very good indeed. The Gobi is one such place. The sands that have preserved the exhumed remains belong to geological periods between the Jurassic and the Oligocene (about 150 to 40 million years ago), that is during the period of mammal evolution into their more specialized forms.

Domestic animals

The domestic animals of the Gobi are sheep and goats, cattle and camels, but the sheep and the goats are by far the most important and number half the livestock population. Cattle number about one-quarter of the population and horses are fewest of all.

The inhabitants of the Gobi have the yak as a domestic animal. In the Gobi Desert the Mongolian herdsmen round up their yaks on horseback. The animal is used for riding, as a beast of burden, and as a milk producer. Domesticated yaks are smaller than the wild ones and interbreed freely with oxen and zebus, producing a docile animal; hybrid males are sterile, the females fertile.

The yak is a horse-tailed ox with cattle horns and a horse's mane. The wild yak lives mainly on high ground in Central Asia, higher than any other species of cattle—between 13,000 and 20,000 feet in Tibet. They are perfectly adapted to this icy environment and are protected from the cold by their warm fur. The yak is a powerful animal about fourteen feet long and standing six feet tall. It has a narrower head than the American bison and

if shorn of its long hair would resemble domestic cattle.

Its horns have a greater spread than those of either American or European bison. They project forward from the head then backwards and are about three feet in length.

The wild yak still exists in Tibet and Kansu, although the present-day wild herds are small. They live in great mountain pastures that could carry many more. Little is known about its life as a wild animal. The domestic animal provides man with meat, tents and other articles. The cows give rich, yellow milk. Even the animal's dung is used for fuel in Mongolia.

The Bactrian, or two-humped camel, is used as a domestic animal from Asia Minor to China. In the Gobi Desert and other parts of Chinese Turkestan, as well as in the Tarim valley, wild Bactrian camels still exist, which may or may not be the descendants of domestic

A lion cub with its mother in the forest of Ghir. These lions show neither animosity nor fear in the presence of human beings and are completely harmless.

A lion resting in the shadows of the Ghir forest watches an approaching hunter. The lions of the Ghir are the last surviving in Asia.

animals that had gone feral in ancient times. In 1957, a herd of Bactrians was discovered in Mongolia near the Altai mountains.

Marco Polo drew attention to the fact that wild camels existed in the heart of Asia and Chinese historians had recorded the fact before Marco Polo's day. The first scientific report was given by Przewalsky, the discoverer of wild horses:

"Finally we saw the wild camels.

We had our camp in a mountain base 10,000 feet above sea level. In the morning we had seventeen degrees of frost and there was an east wind blowing. Suddenly one of the Cossacks noticed a wild camel about 300 paces away. It obviously wanted to go down the pass but after sighting our domestic camels it began to walk towards them. Suddenly it turned in perplexity and ran away. It stopped about fifty paces from our camp and looked back at us, obviously puzzled by the domestic camels. Apparently, it had not understood what it was all about."

Since Przewalsky's time few zoologists have seen a wild camel. Their range has been constantly shrinking and the survivors are now protected by law.

The Bactrian has long been domesticated and is used as a beast of burden as well as providing hides, milk and flesh. But in some ways it is a delicate animal. It stands up well to cold and snowstorms but is not so tolerant of high temperatures. Domestic Bactrians require constant care and attention. On long trips the Bactrian will carry a load of 440 pounds and will cover eighteen miles a day at a slow walk. In some countries there are laws restricting the weight that a camel is allowed to carry.

Wildlife of semi-desert

Argalis are found in the semi-desert areas of Central Asia. In the Altai Gobi region they are active early in the morning and in the evening or during the night and lie up in inaccessible places during the day. In the winter months the animals change their habits, spending all day on foot in their search for food. At this time they form big herds of up to one hundred animals.

The argali is the biggest of all wild sheep, measuring up to six and a half feet long and standing more than four feet tall at the shoulder. A full grown male will weigh 350 pounds or more, the females are smaller and lighter. An old argali ram is like a great muscular athlete. His neck is powerful, his horns massive, sweeping backwards then downwards, then forward to the tip and sometimes making more than a complete turn.

The biggest horns will measure sixty inches round the curve.

Young argalis are born in April and May. The lamb is wobbly on its legs for the first few days of its life, during which time the mother remains with it constantly in rocky places where it can be easily hidden.

The argali is hunted mainly for its massive horns which are of great value. The hides are of little use. In some areas, where they had been killed out completely, they have had to be reintroduced.

Gazelles

The saiga antelope is the ugliest of the gazelles. It is more like a sheep than an antelope and has a large head with a bloated face. It stands about seventeen and a half inches tall and weighs up to one hundred pounds. The species is now found in the Ukraine, Kazakhstan and Mongolia. At the beginning of this century, the saiga was in serious decline but was saved by the Soviet government. There are now half a

A native gamekeeper bearing arms conducts visitors who wish to see the lions of the Ghir. He carries arms in case of emergency but there is no record of the Ghir lions attacking visitors or nomads passing through.

million animals in the Ukraine.

In Mongolia the males gather harems of about forty or fifty and fight fiercely among themselves. Fights to the death appear to be common in this species. During the breeding season the males do not eat but frequently swallow snow. Sometimes they will attack man. After the mating season the males are weak and sometimes mortality is high if the weather becomes severe at that time.

The Mongolian gazelle is found south-east of Altai, and in Mongolia and China at heights varying from 2,000 to 6,000 feet above sea level. This species measures five feet in length and stands between two feet and two feet six inches tall. It weighs about 85 pounds. Formerly the Mongolian gazelle was noted for its considerable migrations which were described by the naturalist, Pallas, as far back as 1776. It seems that these great and regular migrations no longer take place, but in Mongolia there is a southward movement in spring and a movement northwards in autumn.

Such migrations are influenced by the depth of snow and condition of the pastures. Unlike the Persian gazelle, the Mongolian species is highly dependent on water and has to visit watering places regularly—every day in summer and once in every two or three days at other times. This gazelle is an uncommon species in the territory of the Soviet Union, where it is protected by law throughout the year.

The Persian gazelle is found in Turkestan, Mongolia, North West China, Tibet, Persia, in the valley of the Euphrates, in Afghanistan and Baluchistan. There are six races. V. V. Petrov has written of this gazelle:

"This is a typical gazelle, inhabiting desert and semi-desert and rocky and sandy cover with thin vegetation. Sometimes it moves to the forest-covered slopes of moun-

A group of Arati— Mongolian shepherds warmly clad against the cold in the Gobi desert on the border between China and the U.S.S.R. These great camels have two humps and are known as Bactrians. They can stand the great cold of the Gobi but great heat distresses them.

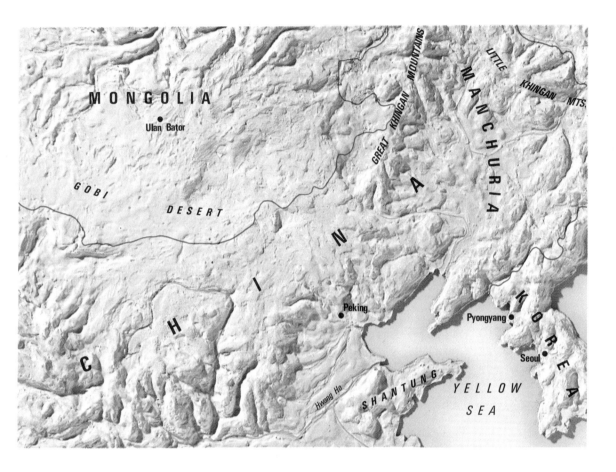

tains and even higher, but it does not live high and is not a mountain species. During the year, Persian gazelles make considerable migrations in search of food, especially during periods of drought. It moves to lower ground in winter and to higher ground in summer. In the Soviet Union, the mating period begins in November or December and lasts about one month. In the second half of April or at the beginning of May the female gives birth to two kids. Single births are exceptional. The kids are helpless at birth and are not able to walk until the third or fourth day. In late summer females and young form large herds and in autumn herds numbering up to 1,000 animals can be seen."

In the Soviet Union hunting of this gazelle is strictly prohibited.

Elsewhere on its range it is killed for food because its meat is of high quality.

Wild horses . . .

Mongolia is the home of the wild horse, not a gone-wild species like the horses that roamed America after the arrival of the Spaniards, but a true wild horse—one of the several ancestors of the domestic horse. It was discovered by the great Russian explorer, Przewalsky, and bears his name: Przewalsky's Horse.

This is the last of the wild horses and was discovered by Przewalsky in 1879. There are still roaming herds of wild Przewalsky's horses living in the wilder parts of the Djungar Steppes and the desert wastes of the Mongolian/Chinese

The Gobi desert is a vast high plain in Mongolia which stretches south into Northern China. It is situated at an altitude varying between 2,500 and 3,500 feet. It is a desert of dunes and rock and salt basins and desolate scrub. It has a cold and very dry climate.

The yak which looks like an ox with a horse's tail is a domestic animal of Mongolia, often used as a pack animal. Here a nomadic shepherd is seen riding a cross-bred yak. The yak is often crossed with other cattle breeds but the hybrids are not so hardy as the pure bred yak.

frontier. In 1959 it was reckoned that the wild horses occupied 8,000 square miles of territory at an altitude of 3,000 to 4,500 feet. Nobody knows just how many of them still exist in these remote regions. In 1959 the Russian, Bannikov, suggested forty, but this is almost impossible to check in a vast, inaccessible territory within which the herds cross and recross between China and Mongolia. According to the latest reports a herd of wild Przewalsky's horses, · numbering forty, was seen in the frontier region of South West Mongolia.

Przewalsky's horse is a small, sturdy animal with a big head. Its summer coat is red and brown, or yellow and brown; in winter it is longer and thicker and greyish-brown in colour. The mane is always straight. In Przewalsky's horse the hair at the root of the tail grows from the sides; in the case of the domestic horse it grows right round the root of the tail.

The wild horse stands between four feet and four feet nine inches high at the shoulder. On its legs there is often a suggestion of black striping. A dark stripe runs along the entire length of the back. Crosses between Przewalsky's horse and the domestic horse are fertile, but crosses with the ass are sterile as with the domestic horse and the ass.

. . . and asses

Asiatic wild asses, or kulans, still roam over the greater part of South and Central Asia—Iraq, Syria, Persia, Baluchistan, Western China, Mongolia, Nepal and Tibet. The kulan is more like a horse than an African ass. It is slimmer than its African relatives and has shorter ears but it still differs from the horse in having a big, rough head, and a tail with hair only in the lower half. The upper part of the body is yellowish brown but the mane is almost totally black. Muzzle, throat, chest, abdomen and the inside of the legs are lighter than the back. A dark stripe runs along the backbone to the tail.

The best known races of the kulan are the Chigetai, Onegar and the Kainj. The chigetai is found in Mongolia and the surrounding area. Onegars are found in Persia, Afghanistan and Turkestan. The kainj is found in Tibet and is the mountain form of the Asiatic ass. It was first described by Przewalsky.

The number of kulans in Asia is dwindling, but the decline is being arrested by protection. In Turkmenistan they have an extensive reservation.

In Mongolia, where kulans are still numerous, only a few animals can be killed each year, probably less than fifty. The decline of the kulan in Mongolia is due not so much to killing as to lack of water, most of which is now used by man. Herds of hundreds can still be seen in small areas of Turkmenistan, in Serach and Kushkin near the Iranian and Afghanistan border. In the U.S.S.R. the hunting of Kulans is absolutely prohibited and severely punished.

The nomads of the Gobi desert have domesticated the tarpan, a species of wild horse. It is a primitive type found only in Mongolia. The Mongolians of the Gobi are expert horsemen, who, seven centuries ago, conquered an immense territory stretching from Bohemia to Vietnam and from Manchuria to Iran.

CHAPTER 5

THE DESERTS
OF AUSTRALIA

One-third of the Australian continent is desert, which means it is the driest country in the world in terms of proportion of desert to total square mileage. But the deserts of Australia are unique because they are the home of plant and animal species found nowhere else in the world. They also had a distinctive human population before the arrival of the white man and a fraction of this native population still exists.

The primitive people, or Aborigines, who lived on the continent before the arrival of white settlers probably numbered about 300,000. Today they number about 110,000, of whom only about 40,000 are pure Aborigines, and of these only a few thousand continue to lead their primitive desert life.

In their struggle for survival the Aborigines became expert hunters and trackers. Indeed they are regarded by many as the finest trackers alive in the world today. Yet they have shown little ability to increase their food supply by the simplest forms of agriculture or by keeping domestic livestock.

On the other hand they have a highly developed social organization and languages of their own. They have a vivid imagination, a fine dramatic sense, and have produced much admirable decorative art. Their lives are ruled by superstition and magic, rites and rituals,

ceremonial and legend. They have their sacred places and acknowledge strange spirits connected with hunting, fishing and medicine. They attempt rainmaking and sorcery.

Probably the best known invention of the Aborigines is the boomerang. When hunting the men use a throwing stick, or woomera, a device for launching spears and quite a different weapon from the boomerang. There are two main types of boomerang—the returnable boomerang, and the hunting, or war weapon. There is a hunting type with a hook at one end which is used for hunting kangaroos. Returning boomerangs are playthings and are mainly used for pleasure.

Gods and myths

In the Aborigine's world there are many gods and many hunting myths. There is a festive dance which is an attempt to ensure a plentiful supply of game. The men of the tribe, decked in feathers and with bodies brightly painted, dance to the accompaniment of bullroarers, which are small, flat, wooden tablets that make a buzzing sound. The tablets are tied to string and whirled in the air by the dancers. The buzzing sound is believed to be a divinity.

Australian Aborigines believe that each man has two souls. When

The eroded slopes of Ayers Rock, south-west of Alice Springs in Central Australia. The vast high plains extending to the west are almost entirely desert very like the Sahara.

a man dies one soul passes to his children while the other returns to the heaven where he lived before he was born. Heaven is filled with mythical god-heroes who take part in fabulous hunts in a world that is an indestructible continuation of the earthly world.

According to the Aborigines the rock paintings and carvings in the desert are the records of their past. It is strange that in so many of the world's deserts, like the Kalahari and the Sahara, the rocks and stones crumbled by the sun are tablets preserving the history of earlier and happier times. They record the time when the desert was still green and the wildlife abundant.

To the Australian Aborigines such a time seems so remote that they do not consider it ever existed. Figures of hunting gods and animals, as well as geometric figures, have now only the most obscure symbolic significance. For the present generation they are signs of magic, treated as though they were the work of spirits rather than people.

Another view of Ayers Rock, a monolith of rose-coloured sand-stone. The perimeter of Ayers Rock measures seven and a half miles.

Today and tomorrow

To the anthropologist the Abo-rigines are not only a link with ancient history — they are living history, the Stone Age men of the twentieth century. Like the wildlife of Australia they were isolated from the rest of the world, and recorded history, like the centuries, passed them by. Now history has caught up with them with much the same impact and results as when it caught up with the Indians of North America.

It is becoming increasingly difficult to study the culture of these native Australians because so few of them now exist uncorrupted by modern man. Many are succumbing to western diseases, and it is thought that some even died because they had lost the will to live. The survivors suffer from a low birth rate and the ties between each new generation and its ancestral way of life become more tenuous.

Some Aborigines are now employed in mines. Some live on government reserves, or mission stations, while others work on sheep and cattle stations. Fewer and fewer remain to pursue the old nomadic way of life in the desert. The nomadic way of life depends on the preservation of the tribal hunting grounds which modern civilized

man keeps invading. The Aborigines retreat into a shrinking living space but have to come to terms with the invader sooner or later. Coming to terms means stepping into the twentieth century and giving up the old ways.

The four deserts

There are four main deserts in Australia: The Gibson, the Great Sandy, the Simpson, and the Great Victoria. On a flight from Adelaide to Alice Springs one passes over end- less stretches of parched earth and scrubland of saltbush and spinifax. Porcupine grass grows in clumps like pincushions, with yellow flower- ing stalks growing out of the base and green shoots when there has been rain.

One hundred years ago the only means of transportation in the desert was the camel, brought to Australia from Arabia to help men to conquer the deserts of this new continent. The pioneers who blazed Australia's desert trails used mainly horses. In 1844, Charles Sturt made

Australian Aborigines look down on an oil well in the heart of the desert area at Ren- ner's Rock. Here ancient men and mod- ern technology can be seen side by side.

An Australian Aborigine painting a hunting scene in the style and technique used by his ancestors to adorn the desert caves and rocks. Despite the pressures of modern civilization many such artists still carry on the ancient tradition.

an expedition to the interior and reached the area where Alice Springs is now. He was accompanied by a Scotsman named John Stuart. In 1858–59, Stuart penetrated far into the desert. He made six expeditions between 1860 and 1862, on the last of which he crossed the entire central desert of Australia, reaching the shores of the Indian Ocean at Van Diemen's Gulf. Other expeditions were going on in other parts of the desert about the same time. An Irish police inspector called Burke and a surveyor named Wills crossed the eastern desert region with two companions in 1861. One member of the expedition died on April 16, 1861. In June, 1861, Burke and Wills died. There was one survivor, a man named King who was saved by an expedition led by the explorer Howitt.

The Simpson

North of Lake Eyre the desert is known as the Simpson. Here there are great areas of clay which becomes ooze after one of the rare falls of rain. Other parts of the desert are known as gibber plains. They are covered with stones of various sizes, some round, some angular. These wind-polished stones are derived from the sandstone and shale of the desert rock. Some of them are bright red, others are reddish brown or reddish purple. Besides the areas of gibber plains there are areas of sand dunes, regular in contour, fifty to a hundred feet high, stretching from horizon to horizon.

Lake Eyre lies near the centre of Australia. Although it is called a lake it is dead and usually dry, the largest of many such lakes. It is really a vast drainage sink, a great salt flat 150 miles long and fifty miles wide. It becomes a true lake of shallow water only rarely in a man's lifetime. Lake Amadeus is another dry lake that holds water only about five times in a century.

A map of the area will show river beds entering the area like veins, but like the lake itself the river courses are dry. In fact the region around Lake Eyre is the driest part of Australia, with a rainfall of less than five inches a year.

Search for water

East of Lake Eyre there are sheep and cattle stations, despite the fact that the vegetation growing here

An Australian Aborigine poses beside examples of his craft —weapons, fetishes and clubs.

differs little from that in most parts of the desert. This is possible because of the great store of water lying under the surface, a store that is fed by run-off from the mountains far to the north east. The area is one of the largest artesian basins in the world and by digging wells the station owners have managed to make water available to their animals in this arid region. In some places this hot water comes to the

surface by its own pressure, providing natural springs which the Australians call Mound Springs.

Despite this large store of underground water, scientists are becoming concerned about the future. The water yield in the last fifty years has been much lower than formerly and some geologists believe that the supply will not be replaced.

Conservationists are also concerned about the march of the desert into areas that once held enough grazing for sheep and cattle. This has been brought about largely by overgrazing. Large numbers of sheep and cattle have cropped the vegetation so hard that soil erosion has resulted, thus transforming areas into sandy desert. Formerly Australia's large rabbit population helped the invasion by the desert, but their numbers have been drastically reduced by the disease known as myxomatosis, so this threat has been largely eliminated.

Near the centre of Australia is the famous Ayers Rock. This is a red sandstone monolith (the largest single piece of stone in the world), $2\frac{1}{4} \times 1\frac{1}{2}$ miles at the base and over 1,000 feet high. In the glare of the sunset it glows as though with internal fire. Ayers Rock is considered to be more than two million years old and is the site of ancient Aboriginal rites and ceremonies.

Not far from Ayers Rock, Mount Olga rises abruptly from the desert. Unlike Ayers Rock, which is composed of fine conglomerate, Mount Olga is composed of coarse-grained boulders and pebbles jointed with silica. When viewed from the top of Ayers Rock, twenty miles distant, Mount Olga looks like a giant pile of large pebbles. Chasms in the huge blocks of stones give lodgment to a variety of plants and trees.

Another great rock of the Australian desert is Mount Connor—a

flat topped mass extending for three miles from east to west and about one mile from north to south. This rock has a sandstone base eaten away by erosion to such an extent that the hard conglomerate on top now overhangs.

Near Alice Springs are many other spectacular land forms such as the Devil's Marbles near Tennant Creek, Stanley Chasm, and Palm Valley. Such areas attract the sight-seer but are still largely uninhabited.

The great interior deserts of Australia result, in part, from their geographical position, in the same way as the Sahara. The Australians refer to these desolate regions as the Outback. We have already noted how the trade winds, blowing from cooler regions into warmer ones, take up moisture from the land they blow over. In Australia the desert acts like a huge mirror, reflecting

Two Aborigines of the Central Australian desert with their battle and hunting weapons. The boomerang, always associated with the Aborigines of Australia, is used nowadays mainly for amusement.

back the sun's heat and causing a mass of dry air to rise from the land. This tends to draw moisture towards the interior but the winds carrying it drop most of it on the mountains bordering the coast, so are dry before they reach the Outback.

An inland sea?

Scientists in Australia had hoped to establish an inland sea in the Great Australian Desert by filling Lake Eyre with salt water from Port Augusta in Spencer's Gulf. The water would be carried by open channel to the southern end of Lake Torrens. Pumps would then lift it into the lake from which it would flow north naturally. If a channel were then cut through the low hills between Lake Torrens and Lake Eyre, water would flow to Lake Eyre by gravity. The salt water would then be changed to fresh to make plants grow. So much for the idea. The project had to be given

A group of Aborigine children from a village in the northern part of the continent.

An Australian Aborigine of the Northern desert playing the musical wind instrument known as a didgeridoo.

up because of the high loss of water by evaporation. The project remains one of the great might-have-beens.

Wildlife

Much of the animal life of Australian deserts lives underground and is thus difficult to observe, but a waterhole is a good place to see other species. Nelly's Hole in Ayers Rock is interesting for this reason. This is a permanent waterhole and attracts kangaroos, smaller marsupials, large birds like emus, and many other animals.

Kangaroos are probably the most widely known of Australian mammals. Being grazing animals they are found in areas where man has now established cattle and sheep. Kangaroos are marsupials, which means that the young grow from an early stage in their development in a pouch in the mother's skin. The young kangaroo suckles there, hides there, and is carried there until it is self supporting.

A well known carnivore, the dingo, is a member of the dog family, much persecuted by sheepmen and now rather rare. The origin of the dingo is uncertain but it is thought to be the descendant of a domesticated type taken into Australia by the Aborigines.

Another desert species found only in Australia is the marsupial mole. Like the kangaroo it carries its young in a marsupium, or pouch. Apart from this distinction, the marsupial mole in other ways resembles the mole of the northern hemisphere. Its claws are designed for digging out the insects that bury themselves deeply in the desert sands. The moles come out only during rainy, or cloudy weather.

One does not usually expect to find frogs in the desert because they are moisture-loving creatures. But in the deserts of Australia there are some species that can withstand droughts of a year or more. One of these stores water in its urinary bladder and body cavity so that it looks like a ball. Once it is thus prepared it goes underground to await the next rainfall. After the next heavy rain the frogs come out and are active and noisy in the temporary pools. After such rain, birds, reptiles, and insects also appear and flowers turn the prevailing red of the desert sands into into a patchwork of colour.

Man and natural resources

In Australia, as in other parts of

Flood water in the desert of the Nullarbor plain. At one time this vast expanse of arid land was covered by the sea.

the world, man has not always been a good manager of natural resources because he has ignored or been unaware of the upsets that can follow disruption of natural balance or destruction of habitats. Australians, like everybody else, are becoming more conscious of their responsibilities and keep them in mind when trying new ways of exploiting nature's bounty. A sophisticated programme of pasture management is correcting the mistakes of the past and even in the exploitation of mineral resources thought is given to the effect on the total environment.

The first Australians, the an-

cestors of today's Aborigines, contrived to live through the centuries without unduly upsetting their environment. Like primitive peoples elsewhere their way of life prevented the overharvesting of any natural resource. We live in an age of massive exploitation of natural resources, which is why modern man has achieved massive disasters on a scale no primitive people could have accomplished.

But the way of life of the Aborigines evolved by trial and error through the centuries would not be acceptable to modern man. In times of food shortages the Aborigines suffered from malnutrition. Being

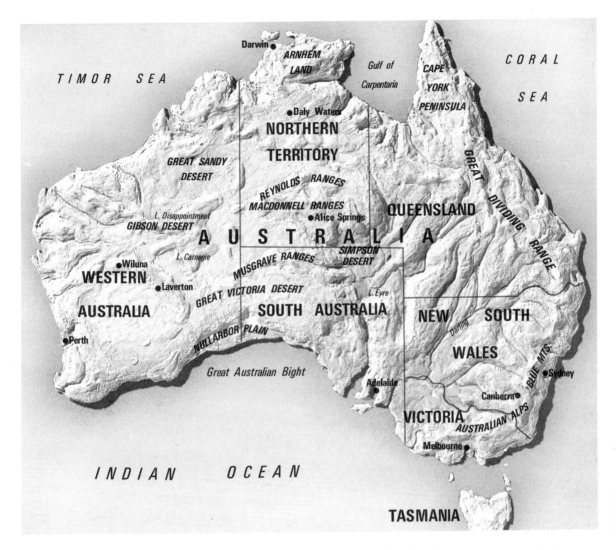

Map labels:
TIMOR SEA
Darwin
ARNHEM LAND
Gulf of Carpentaria
CAPE YORK PENINSULA
CORAL SEA
Daly Waters
NORTHERN TERRITORY
GREAT SANDY DESERT
REYNOLDS RANGES
MACDONNELL RANGES
QUEENSLAND
GREAT DIVIDING RANGE
L. Disappointment
GIBSON DESERT
Alice Springs
A U S T R A L I A
SIMPSON DESERT
L. Carnegie
MUSGRAVE RANGES
Wiluna
WESTERN
Laverton
GREAT VICTORIA DESERT
L. Eyre
SOUTH AUSTRALIA
NEW
SOUTH
AUSTRALIA
Perth
NULLARBOR PLAIN
Darling
WALES
BLUE MTS
Sydney
Great Australian Bight
Adelaide
Canberra
VICTORIA
AUSTRALIAN ALPS
Melbourne
INDIAN   OCEAN
TASMANIA

nomads whose life depended on their mobility, they would leave the infirm and the old and even unwanted children behind at waterholes when they became a hindrance. However much modern man admires the Aborigines' will and ability to survive under the harshest conditions, the whole modern outlook rejects the consequences of such a life.

Australia is a land rich in mineral resources, mainly on the perimeter of the deserts. Inaccessibility creates a problem but modern science is finding ways to solve it. There are billions of tons of iron ore and large deposits of copper, silver, gold, lead,

and other minerals in the desert areas. Exploiting these has meant the digging of harbours and the building of railroads through the rough terrain to the source. But the scientists try to keep in mind their responsibilities to the total environment.

The trial-and-error method of maintaining balance, developed by the Aborigines through the centuries, is being replaced by careful planning based on modern research. Modern man is becoming more and more aware of the interaction of the many forces of the natural world. Even in a desert nature cannot be ignored.

In Australia there are wide expanses of desert — the Great Sandy desert, the Gibson desert, the Victoria desert and the Simpson, which occupy about a third of the country.

CHAPTER 6

THE DESERTS OF AMERICA

The deserts of North America are not all alike. Some of them have their special plant and animal communities which, though not exclusive to them, are characteristic. There is also a great variation of climate. They have features in common with the deserts of Africa and Asia — hot sun, dust, and sand dunes, but they also have features of their own. The great authority of North American deserts, Edmund C. Jaeger, believes that anyone with an intimate knowledge of all parts of the North American deserts will have a good understanding of desert climates in other parts of the world.

The Mojave Desert of California has hot, dry summers and cool, relatively moist winters. The low-lying Sonoran Desert is in the western half of the Mexican state of Sonora and extends into Southern Arizona, South-east California and the north-east corner of Lower California. This desert consists of broad, sandy, and rocky plains more or less enclosed by mountains. This vast arid region extends to nearly 120,000 square miles and has been divided into six major areas, including the famous Colorado Desert of California. There is considerable variation of landscape as well as plant and animal life in the Sonora.

The Colorado Desert is the closest American parallel to the hot deserts of the Old World; its driest parts are as dry as the driest areas of the Sahara. Most of the Colorado has mild winters, very hot summers, and in some areas a climate similar to that of Western Pakistan.

The part of the Sonoran desert that slopes towards the Gulf of California has a marked concentration of rainfall in the hot season and is much like the Thar desert of Pakistan and India where there is a brief monsoon season. This type of climate is also found in the northern, tropical part of the Australian desert.

The Grand Canyon

One of the most spectacular sights in the world is the Grand Canyon area of Arizona where the Colorado River has scoured through layer after layer of rock so that it is now flowing about a quarter of a mile deeper than its bed of a million years ago. The lower canyon walls are still desert but the higher ground of the Colorado Plateau, through which it flows, is humid enough to support trees. Unlike most desert rivers, which peter out short of the sea or other body of water, the Colorado neither begins nor ends in the desert: it merely travels through desert areas on its way to the sea. It is thus an exception to the rule about desert rivers.

The rocky tower of Castleton, typical of rock formations in the desert of Utah, was produced by wind erosion.

One of the most famous beauty spots in the state of Utah is Bryce Canyon. Here, pink towers of fantastic shapes stand as memorials to a past age when the ancient rivers eroded away all the softer rock. Mineral oxides tint the rock and make it a beautiful sight, especially when the sun is shining on it.

The salt flats

In contrast with this there are the Bonneville Salt Flats. Here the salt deposits left behind after the evaporation of water are estimated at a million tons. Each spring the rain dissolves salt from the rocks of the mountains as it flows to the Bonneville levels and more salt is left there when the water evaporates.

In New Mexico there is the famous Tularosa Basin—a large area of white gypsum. Here the gypsum crystals are formed by evaporation, in much the same way as the salt crystals are formed in the Bonneville Flats. The wind grinds the gypsum crystals into sand-like particles and piles them in dunes. The most beautiful crystals can be seen in the White Sands National Monument.

The biggest desert in America is the Great Basin Desert which covers most of Nevada and Utah, parts of Wyoming, Idaho and Oregon, a small corner of Colorado, and a good piece of California. This is a region of endless miles of sagebrush, salt bush, and greasewood. The Great Basin is defined as a cold desert, which means that it has fewer burning hot days than truly hot deserts and has more moisture than the surrounding areas. The Great Basin is high ground, rising from 2,000 to as high as 6,000 feet above sea level and much of it is salty.

The deserts of North America lie between the Rocky Mountains and the Sierra Nevada. The most spectacular is the desert of Arizona which covers most of the Colorado plain—a vast tableland of rock layers through which the river has cut a deep channel — the Grand Canyon.

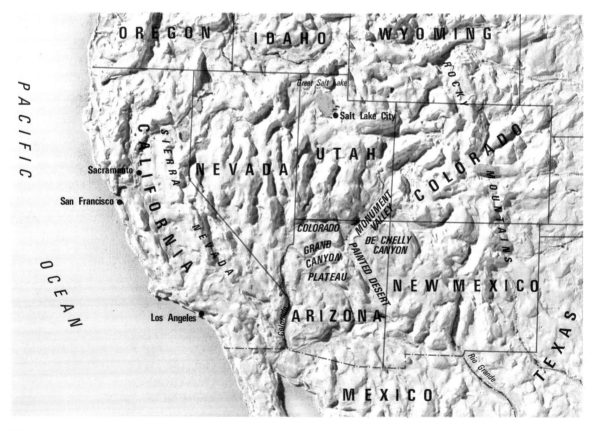

Modern America in the desert

American deserts, besides having much in common with those of Africa and Asia, have features that are unique—great modern highways cutting across them, motels, signposts, advertising hoardings, electric and telegraph lines. The white vapour trails of jet aircraft are a common sight in the sky. Buses travel along the roads unloading gaily clad tourists in search of the desert. All these signs indicate that the American deserts have been conquered. It is now possible to cross the entire Arizona desert by motor car in about eight hours. Tourism in the American deserts is such that conservationists are becoming concerned about the future and are seeking legislation to protect something of America's remaining desert wilderness.

But tourists arc visitors. What of people who actually live in the desert? These are now few and they are Indians, many of whom still live a nomadic life. They are the remnants of the Navajo, Apache and Sioux, the descendants of the Red Men who fought and lost the battle against the white invaders.

The natives

The inland desert region of the Colorado Plateau is the land of the Navajo. The entire plateau is an arid tableland of piled strata made up of sedimentary rock, layer upon layer. Here is the famous Monument Valley of walls and towers and pinnacles, carved into the most extravagant forms by that most capricious of desert artists, the wind. In this area, on a great rectangle of grassland, steppe, and desert, about 220 by 120 miles, live the Navajo. This is their reserve which

Monument Valley in the Arizona desert, the reservation of the Navajo Indians, is one of the famous show pieces of the United States of America and is preserved as a national monument.

they share with some Hopi and Apache. There are a few populated centres on this reserve. Monument Valley is one of the few.

Here the Navajo live, true to themselves and their traditions. Unlike so many other tribes who, in their long wars with the white man, were either pacified, or exterminated, or reduced to a few miserable decadent groups, the Navajo have established an efficient social organization within their community—a community settled in the most fascinating of all the American desert lands.

Here in this community the name of Kit Carson, the famous American scout, lives on in the memory of the Navajo like that of a New World Genghiz Khan. In 1863, after his epic journey across the desert, Carson attacked the Navajo at Canyon de Chelly. He destroyed their villages in the green areas that dotted the arid plain like oases. He blocked up the wells and destroyed the irrigation canals, thus destroying the basis of their livelihood. Their crops and trees died and it seemed that extinction must overtake the Navajo as it had so many other Indian tribes. Many were taken captive, put in camps, or were transported to the western part of New Mexico. But the remainder, now no more than 12,000, succeeded in rebuilding their social life and their ethnic unity. Today the Navajo number about 60,000.

The culture of the Navajo is expressed in their "sand paintings" which are not paintings at all but polychrome symbols in the sand. They are representations of the forces of nature, expressions of the relationship between the Navajo and a superior spirit. God, demigod, or hero, this being is for the Navajo the reflection of all perfection, the goal of his aspirations.

The Navajo dwelling is called a *hogan*, and even when built of masonry follows the classical form of the Indian tepee. The materials have changed but the outline has remained intact. Some of the hogans are ancient, so in this community there is a mixture of dwellings, ancient and modern. In the older type the ceiling is of branches and poles, exactly like a tepee. The chimney, built in traditional style, is

in the centre and the smoke escapes through a hole in the top. Before winter sets in, earth, sand and stones are placed over the holes and on the branches to protect the inmates from the cold. The hogans, old and new, fit into the flat landscape of sand and rocks and grey-black sky.

Albert Camus wrote of this desert: "Mountains of rock and ice frame these American deserts; they stop the rain-laden winds and hew out a visible frontier in the sky between winter and eternal summer, between water and stone. They were not fed by the rains, so the torrents dried up and the soil became corrugated. The water disappeared into the muddy bottoms or evaporated to form these brief morning clouds which the rising sun dries up from the hollows in the ground before baking the rocks and sand. And thus the scorching ground is covered by

Sunset in the Colorado. This great desert, south-west of the Rocky Mountains, is a vast tableland. The cacti in the foreground are typical of American deserts.

Navajo Indians at work on one of their
famous paintings in the sand.

a vast dry layer, hardened here and there by salt deposits, or undulating petrified waves of former oceans. In the hollows of these waves life is visible only through its traces. The desert, like a coagulated memory of the world, offers its fossilized imprints, mineral shadows of vanished species or rocky spectres of the forest where history had its beginning. Only the stones and the sand remain and it is difficult to understand what invisible force moved them."

Plants and animals

Great areas of the North American deserts provide homes for a wide variety of plant and animal life adapted to living in dry regions. Although the desert may seem silent and empty, it is really very much alive. There is much activity, especially in the cool of the day and during the night. Even in Death Valley, where some of the highest temperatures on earth have been recorded, there are twelve species of lizards, 600 species of plants, and about thirty species of mammals.

The cacti

Though some kinds of plants and animals are common to a variety of deserts, the deserts of America are unique because of their cactus plants. These plants, native only to the Americas, appear in a great variety of forms. Some are barrel-shaped; some, like the teddy-bear cholla, are small, soft and fuzzy; and some are large like the saguaro, the king of the cactuses, fifty feet tall and ten tons or more in weight. The great saguaro sometimes forms whole forests covering many acres. These giant cacti have a root spread of about 35 feet in all directions. The roots act as an anchor during high winds and enable the plants to gather large quantities of water after rain.

The saguaro is a slow grower which begins its life in the shade of another plant. At ten years of age the young cactus is only four inches tall. At twenty-five years it is two feet tall and it is fifty years old before it reaches a height of six feet. In a century the plant will reach thirty-five feet.

The saguaro is a source of food to many desert species. Mice, rats and weevils feed on the seedlings and the fruit is eaten by men and animals. The barrel cactus also provides food for animals and birds and because of its capacity to hold moisture provides water for many animals including man.

Here, as in other deserts, plants and animals have to contend with chronic water shortage. The cacti store water which is sought after by a variety of animals. The cactus plants have to protect themselves against browsing and they do so by means of their barbed needles. But the protection is not total although it does save the plants from being destroyed. The result is that cacti and animals manage to live together and the plants have a wonderful capacity to recover even after a heavy attack. Besides food and water, some species provide nesting places for birds. The cholla, for example, is a favourite nesting place of wrens.

Some American deserts have plants typical of them—plants that grow in profusion in one desert and are rare and absent in others. The century plant, which is highly drought resistant, is characteristic of the Mojave-Colorado desert of California. Sagebrush is the characteristic plant of the Great Basin desert.

A plant common to many Ameri-

Giant cactus and rainbow in the Arizona desert.

A train travelling across the most barren South-American desert between the Cordillera of the Andes and the Pacific coast. . .

The train crosses the savanna zone before entering the barren land of the Atacama desert.

Villagers at home near the southern edge of the Atacama desert between Peru and Chile.

of leaves enables the plant to conserve moisture by preventing transpiration. Many desert plants manage to survive in this way, among them the palo verde and crucifix thorn. The palo verde with its yellow blossom grows in dry gullies and taps water lying a few feet below ground. The mesquite, on the other hand, will send its roots as far as one hundred feet down to tap deeper water.

Annual plants on the desert burst suddenly into bloom as though by magic and this is because they respond quickly to conditions that ensure their survival. Their seeds lie dormant and do not germinate until conditions are right, which means they lie dormant during the dry weather and germinate only after rain. But the moisture must be abundant enough to give the plant time to flower and produce seeds for the future. Some annuals bloom after winter rain and some after summer rain, but all of them must have the right quantity of rain at the right time. The purplemat is an annual with such a compressed life cycle.

can deserts is the creosote bush which gets its name from the smell of its leaves. This bush is highly drought resistant. It sheds its leaves, twigs and even whole branches during a dry spell and, to the casual observer, appears to be completely dead. But live buds remain hidden ready to come to life at the first rainfall. The creosote bush then produces leaves and yellow blossom. This bush is found over millions of acres of the American deserts.

Another plant that sheds its leaves during drought is the ocotillo. It comes to life after rain and produces scarlet flowers. The shedding

Rare species

The deserts of America are the habitat of many species of wildlife. One of the most fascinating (the very spirit of the desert it has been called), is the Kit Fox whose fur matches the desert sand. The kit fox hunts at dawn and dusk, preying to a very great extent on kangaroo rats. Unfortunately, the kit fox is becoming rare. It lacks the wariness we usually associate with foxes, so is easily trapped. Poison baits laid down for coyote and other predators are eaten by kit foxes. So poison is another threat to its survival.

Another threatened species is the

desert Bighorn sheep which survives now on federal refuges in Arizona and Nevada, but poaching is still a serious problem and a threat to the bighorn's existence. The Gila monster, the only poisonous lizard in the world, is also rare as the result of constant persecution. It exists in Arizona where it is now protected.

The Pronghorn antelope is not found outside North America. Two centuries ago it could be numbered in millions. Twenty years ago it was threatened with extinction. It was rescued by State and Federal agencies and by private bodies like the National Audubon Society. Groups of wild pronghorns still exist in places like the Painted Desert but their real refuges today are in the Charles Sheldon Antelope Refuge of Nevada, and the Hart Mountain National Antelope Refuge in Oregon, from which animals have been sent to build up herds elsewhere in the United States and Canada.

Dry feeding

The Kangaroo Rat is one of the commonest and most fascinating desert animals. Despite the fact that it lives in the hot desert it cannot stand great heat and if exposed to high daytime temperatures for any length of time it would die. It solves this problem by staying underground during the hottest part of the day and coming out late. So it has no difficulty in combating the heat. It has also little difficulty with the problem of water scarcity: it just does not drink. Yet it feeds mainly on dry seeds which contain little or no water.

It manages all this by a highly evolved system of water concentration. It loses no moisture by panting or sweating. Its urine is so

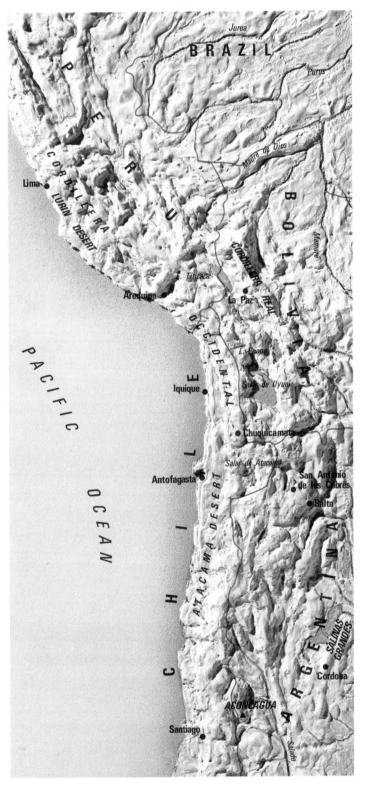

The deserts of South America form a narrow band along the coasts of Peru and Chile at the foot of the Andes. The most extensive is the Atacama desert of Northern Chile.

concentrated that little water is lost in getting rid of body wastes. And it uses metabolic water. The sugar in its food breaks down to release hydrogen and oxygen which combine to make this metabolic water. In most other animals metabolic water is useless to maintain body fluids but the kangaroo rat, having reduced its loss of body fluid, can make do with the small amount of metabolic water derived from dry seeds.

The Screech owl is a bird of the desert and a night hunter. It preys on mice, insects, lizards and other animals, and nests in holes in the giant saguaro cactus. The saguaro is necessary to this owl's existence. The bird that provides the holes in the cactus is the Gila woodpecker, and birds other than owls use such holes—sparrowhawks, flickers, and flycatchers.

Coyotes and cattle

Perhaps the best known and most talked about desert animal is the Coyote—a night hunter and predator on rats, and much persecuted by man. The howling of the coyote, much loved by songwriters, is not a pleasing sound to the ears of the cattleman who constantly persecutes this animal.

The cattleman has played his part in changing the face of some American deserts and causing unforeseen chain reactions. Until 1870 the South-West had few cattle, then hundreds of thousands were brought in to feed on the tough desert grasses growing among the cactus, mesquite and other desert plants. Within twenty years the region was suffering from overgrazing. Then there was a severe drought. The drought in itself would not have damaged the desert vegetation but overgrazing by cattle had bared the soil which became badly eroded during the drought. This resulted in an increase of cholla and prickly pear cacti and a decrease in the saguaros. The grasses needed by the young saguaros no longer existed and they died for want of nurse plants. They died for another reason. Wood rats increased in number with the cholla and prickly pear and began to destroy saguaro seedlings. The wood rat was in turn helped by men who persisted in trying to eradicate its main enemy, the coyote.

There are at least twelve species of rattlesnake in the North American deserts, the largest being the Diamond-back which grows to a length of six feet. All rattlesnakes are venomous but the diamond-back is considered the most deadly. Another species well known by repute is the Sidewinder which crawls diagonally and leaves a distinctive J-track in the sand. Other members of this notable family are the Fer-de-Lance and the Moccasin snake.

South America

The great deserts of South America are the Atacama-Peruvian of 140,000 square miles in Chilean-Peru, and the Patagonian of 260,000 square miles in Argentina. The Atacama-Peruvian has the lowest rainfall in the world—less than half an inch a year on average. The Patagonian desert closely resembles the Sonoran because many of the plant species are identical.

One part of the Atacama is a desert within a desert, an area which scientists call an absolute desert. There is only one other such place in the world and that is in the Sahara. The Atacama's desert-within-a-desert is isolated and harsh, with a rainfall so slight that in a twenty-year period it amounted to only one inch. In one part of this area, barely eighty miles from the Pacific Ocean, no one remembers rain ever falling.

But despite its extreme aridity the Atacama is a cloudy desert. Fog hangs above many parts of the coastal region and although this rarely falls as rain it allows plants and animals to live. In this dismal desert the skies are grey for about six months of the year and the land is obscured by mists that give way to sunshine only during the summer months. And then the sunshine is very hot.

Here, as elsewhere, the commonest animals are burrowers. Surface temperatures are often extremely high so the animals dig beneath the surface where the temperature is lower and relatively constant. Some live in holes or cracks in the rocks where they are insulated against the sun's heat. Rodents burrow into mounds covered by vegetation. The vegetation is scant and scattered but survives to provide shelter and food for rodents.

In some parts of the Peruvian desert there are areas of vegetation where the winter mists prevent rapid evaporation of moisture. This allows many plant species to flower for a brief season, covering large areas with yellow blossom. Areas of vegetation are known as *Lomas* by the people of Peru and were farmed many years ago by early civilized peoples. But even the lomas dry up at the beginning of summer when moisture from the mists is no longer present.

The fog over the Atacama-Peruvian desert is caused by the Peru current and that over the Southern Patagonian desert by the Falkland Current. These are cold water currents, like rivers flowing through the sea, sweeping along the coast. The winds that blow over these currents can carry little moisture and what they carry becomes fog that only rarely condenses to become water.

Photograph of a condor, the great vulture of the Andes desert regions, photographed by means of a telephoto lens.

Indians of the Chilean desert of South America.

91

CHAPTER 7

THE SAHARA

The Sahara, spanning the 4,375 miles between the Atlantic Ocean and the Red Sea is the biggest desert in the world. From the Mediterranean it stretches southwards for 1,562 miles. It covers an area of three and a half million square miles. This enormous land surface is divided among many modern sovereign states — Morocco, Algeria, Tunis,. Niger, Mauritania, Libya, Egypt, Chad, Mali, the Sudan and part of Nigeria. Spanish Sahara still remains under the colonial administration of Spain.

Although the Sahara is a single great desert it is subdivided on the map into smaller areas, including the Libyan, Téneré, and the Desert of Bayuda. The name Sahara is usually reserved for the Central and Western area. There are mountain ranges in the central region: the Adrar Des Iforas, the Air, the Hoggar, the Ennedi, and the Tibesti which reaches a height of 10,000 feet above sea level. There is also a great lake in the area, Lake Chad, which is almost exactly the size of Wales. The region is rich in mineral resources, petroleum, iron, phosphates, copper, manganese, platinum and uranium.

There is not an acre of the Sahara on which more than 100 millimetres of rain have fallen in any year during the last century, and there are many parts that have less than that.

Adrar in Southern Algeria has no more than 12.7 mm in any year. The average for Kharga in the Egyptian desert is 1.1 mm. Dakka in the same area has an absolute limit of .4 mm of rain a year.

Automatic meteorological stations are now being set up in many parts of the Sahara as links in a world-wide chain of weather stations. From these automatic stations the collected data will be passed by radio teletype to the main world centres in Washington, Moscow and Melbourne, thus helping to give a more complete world weather picture. Everyone knows that the Sahara is dry, that other parts of the world are wet, and others almost permanently frozen, but the study of weather is not a parochial one. To study the complex causes of weather the meteorologist has to work on a world scale and that includes the deserts.

Green Sahara

"Dry as the Sahara" is a synonym commonly in use. To most people, to everyone indeed, the name means a furnace of heat and wind and blown sand. Yet this great area was not always as dry as it is today. The geological record makes it clear that at one time conditions were quite different. Regions that are now among the driest in the world were

A jeep makes its way over the undulating sands of the Sahara. This is the trackless erg region.

Terracotta model of a nomad's camel from the Chad region of the Sahara.

watered, in prehistoric times, by great rivers.

Today there are seas of sand that were once great lakes. Lake Chad was probably a freshwater sea with a coastline eight times longer than now. On the shores of this sea lived many animal species; hippopotamuses, rhinoceroses, and crocodiles among them.

In those days great tracts of the Sahara were green and lush with vegetation, and the evidence suggests that shepherds were herding their flocks there as recently as 5,000 years ago. The climate was temperate and the vegetation supported great flocks of sheep. These ancient people have left countless records, in engravings and carvings, of life there in those far-off times, and there is good reason to believe that overgrazing by sheep helped to make the Sahara the desert it is today.

Long before the days of the shepherds and their flocks (perhaps as long as 350,000,000 years ago), parts of the desert were covered by the ocean. Near the Southern border of Libya there are rocky outcrops that were once probably a chain of islands. These peaks, known as the Aguilles de Sissé, are all that remain of a great plateau 1,000 feet high. When the ocean dried up, the plateau became exposed to the action of wind and rain. At that time the region was wetter than it is today. Weathering gradually eroded the rocks so that the plateau disintegrated until only hard peaks remained to become spires in a sea of sand. They are a strange and beautiful sight.

Romantic desert

This silver cross of Coptic origin is in the possession of a nomadic tribe in the Nubian desert.

The Sahara more than any other desert has inspired explorers, writers, scientists, adventurers, film makers, ethnographers, romantics in search of solitude, and mystics in search of God. It is the desert of the great sand dunes where camel caravans move in fretted silhouette against the sky; the desert of Beau Geste and the French Foreign Legion; the desert of the nomadic Blue Men—the legendary Tuaregs —who long terrorized those who lived or travelled in the desert. It is now the desert of the oil prospectors, forever searching for deposits that could be the greatest in the world.

Some of these images are images of yesterday. What remains of them today?

The Foreign Legion has disappeared, leaving only relics of a bygone age, not least the French language. The silence of the dunes remains except that it is more and more frequently broken by the noise of the internal combustion engine. Inexorably, technology is moving into the desert. More and more scientists and adventurers explore the wastes in search of petroleum and other mineral deposits that could make this desert richer than the richest sheikdom of Arabia.

The pressure of events, the invasion of technology, contact with new customs and outlooks, are gradually eroding away the customs of the nomadic peoples, who are slowly changing their ways with the times. Yet still, in its vastness the Sahara retains its aura of mystery, attracting the adventurer of today as it did the adventurer of yesterday.

Music of the dunes

Suppose you were to take a trip by truck or jeep through the Sahara from north to south. One of your first experiences would probably be listening to the "drums of the dunes". This takes place at night,

when the wind is icy cold and your fingers freeze on the steering wheel.

You are preparing for the night and have built a small fire with a few rags soaked in petrol and some wooden boards from an empty box. Your guide says this is the best moment to listen to the *Tobol*, or drums of the dunes.

But before you can hear the music produced by these great expanses of yellow sand you have to wait until your ears have recovered from the revving of the motor engine and are attuned to the silence of the desert. You have to become part of the silence, surrender yourself to the solitude, for only then can you hear the *tobol*.

The fire dies, the night is silent and dark, and you experience no sensation other than the peace and quiet and total solitude of the desert. You move away from the road and climb on to the packed sand of the dune. There you put your ears to the ground and wait patiently, quietly, almost without breathing. You lie prone on the sand and listen. The wind blowing

Nomads watering their camels at a drinking place on the southern edge of the Sahara desert between the Ennedi mountains and the Chad/Sudan border. Watering places like this are vital to the existence of man and beast.

The ruins of a Roman city in Sabratha in Libya. The columns and antique murals of the ancient capital can be seen.

A mosaic discovered during an archaeological excavation in the desert of Southern Tunisia.

on the undulating crests of the dunes raises thousands of minute sand grains from the higher regions. The grains are swept far away. Even inside the dunes the mass of sand becomes unsettled and everything seems to move above and below.

With your ears against the ground you become conscious of this almost imperceptible, indefinite, but continuous unseen movement. The dunes, like harmonic chords, multiply and repeat the notes of the rustling, shifting sands. In contrast to the surrounding absolute silence you now hear what sounds like the sonorous rhythmic music of distant drums, roll after roll, after roll. The sound has a constant pattern, a strange rhythm unlike any sound you are ever likely to hear in the everyday world. Such is the *tobol,* the legendary music of the singing dunes, a rhythm rather than a sound.

Trackless wastes

On the journey towards the centre of the Sahara you have to traverse three regions, each with characteristics found in parts of other deserts of the world, and each a hazard to the most experienced traveller. There are Ergs, or great expanses of undulating sand dunes; Hammadas which are flat, rocky barrens; and Chotts or expanses of salt that blind with their brightness.

On such a journey the jeep is still the only mechanical means of transport that can compete with the camels of the nomads. Navigation by compass of the kind used for navigation at sea becomes obligatory. At sea, ships sail from country to country, navigating by compass and take into account such factors as storms and changing currents. Here in the desert one has to navigate from oasis to oasis, mindful of

the shifting sand and the changing contours.

Wastes with tracks

During a trip through the desert you will come across all sorts of roads—roads that are little more than the tortuous windings of wheel tracks along the dunes; paths like corrugated paper on the imperceptibly undulating terrain; uncertain mountain paths. There are, of course, two-lane roads where it is possible to drive at considerable speed. There are small passages that cut through the overhang of the

Hoggar crags of the Central Sahara. There are tracks, barely visible, worn on the stones of the hammadas by the caravans over the centuries. There are great stretches where road or trail has been obliterated by windblown sand and where only the straight lines of telegraph poles, stretching from horizon to horizon, mark the way. Some of these poles extend in a straight line for many miles and are used even by aeroplane pilots to check their course.

Of course it is a simple matter nowadays to reach even the remotest part of the desert by air, and many such trips are made by oil

The ruins of the magnificent amphitheatre of El Djem in Southern Tunisia. In Roman times this was a grain producing area; now wind and sand have taken over and the productive fields no longer exist. The Roman amphitheatre was once the centre of a well populated province on this sunbaked desert plateau.

company planes and by military and private aircraft flying from oasis to oasis and village to village. But if one wishes to see the Sahara as it really is, to experience at first hand its glamour, its hostility, and its hazards, the jeep is still the only alternative to the camel.

A jeep can travel along the communication networks built by oil prospectors, or follow the many long pipelines that cross the desert. But anyone who wishes to leave the most populated or most frequented regions to explore areas least touched by technological civilization, must use the secondary roads.

A pump attendant fills the traveller's petrol tank at a filling station in the Central Algerian Sahara.

Desert traffic jams

One of the strange sights in the desert is a traffic light and one can be seen at the oasis of In-Salah. Here the new Africa—the Africa of jeeps, trucks and oil prospectors —can be seen alongside the old Africa, the Africa of the Tuaregs

with their camels and the Bedouins with their donkeys. All wait for the red light to change to green.

It is a busy scene, almost a traffic jam, yet on both sides of the traffic light lies the most immense solitude in the world. Near oases, and on the desert fringe, one will see vegetation and shrubs and nomads and their tents, and perhaps a view of mountain peaks beyond the horizon. But out on the erg there is nothing in sight, no life, no movement. It is a featureless land of changing contours where one feels as though one is moving in a vacuum.

There are places marked on the desert map as though they were towns or cities, whereas they may be no more than centres with a few inhabitants—perhaps merely supply centres, where piles of empty oil drums lie scattered and full drums are stacked in geometric mountains. There may be only one man in the place, the watchman who stands guard. He is a solitary figure with a

A vehicle makes its way along a typical Saharan road — a lonely road in one of the loneliest and emptiest parts of the world.

An Arab boy beside the oasis of El Golea in the Algerian Sahara. The green of the oasis stands out against the yellow of the sand. The rocks are like islands in a sea of sand.

The kanaga mask is used by people of the desert zones of Occidental Mali in Africa. The mask is worn during religious rain dances.

tween Buttafal in Chad and the first well of Kufra in Libya. In this part of the world the caravans ply between North Chad, the sub-Libyan desert and the Ennedi mountains of North-east Chad, carrying on most of their trade between oasis and oasis and village and village. The journey from Buttafal to Kufra is 187 miles with not a well or a blade of grass between. This trail is called the Silk Road, a trail of sand where the feet sink up to the ankles at every step. Yet the nomads cover it in seven days, carrying all their water with them.

In the old days the nomads set their course by the stars because there were no other points of reference, but nowadays they find it much easier to be guided by aircraft. There is a daily flight by Air France along the route and the aircraft can be seen in the sky at a certain time each night. The regularity of the flight means that it can be relied on as a time check and the plane's navigation lights, clearly visible on a good night, act as a star to steer by. The plane's direction of travel can be noted and it is much easier to follow it than to navigate by the stars. As a result the number of nomads capable of crossing the unmarked desert unaided is becoming smaller and smaller.

rifle in one hand and a petrol pump in the other, waiting to supply travellers with petrol. Bidon V in Southern Algeria is one such petrol station in the desert. It is at such times that dimensions of tens of thousands of square miles of emptiness begin to have real meaning.

The silk road

Suppose you met a caravan in the Tibesti region of the Chad and asked one of the nomads; which is the most difficult trail in the whole of the Sahara—he and any other member of the caravan would give a unanimous answer: the trail be-

The nomads who travel the Silk Road are agreed on the greatest single danger of this most difficult journey. Towards the end of the trip, they say, it needs only a small error of judgment to make them miss the oasis and its well. The oasis is not visible at any great distance and even the smallest miscalculation could make them bypass the place where the water is.

Here are the symbols of desolation and death on the edge of the Algerian Sahara. The bones scattered about the sand are of camels that died of thirst in this parched land. Nearby are the ruins of a Roman aqueduct that once carried water to this thirsty land.

Water, water . . .

If a nomad becomes lost he might

in desperation be driven to drink from an unknown well with bad water. Although he would tell you that nomads like himself can hold out for a long time without water — and this is true — no man can live without it beyond a certain time. It is when this time approaches that the nomad may be forced to drink unsuitable water. Such water not only has an unpleasant taste; it causes nausea and diarrhoea and this can be extremely dangerous in the desert. In rare cases the water may contain harmful salts. On one occasion some of the men of a caravan used the water from an unknown well to wash in. Their hands became blistered with sores that lasted thirty days. The younger people of the caravan, who had not been warned in time, drank a little of the water and were extremely ill.

Men working in the Sahara may be rationed to two gallons of water per day and it is possible to walk twenty miles on one gallon of water if the walking is done only at night. So, in fact, it is possible to exist for twenty-four hours on half the normal ration. Much depends on the temperature during the day, for the

A lost traveller encounters two Maharisti nomads on the dunes of the Oriental Saharan erg and seeks their help and direction.

hotter it is the more water one loses by perspiration. Naturally, travelling in the desert is much more pleasant if one's water supply is not so limited.

In desert travel it is important never to underestimate the amount of water you will require. Knowing the number of miles you have to travel to the next supply does not always tell you how many hours it will take you to get there. And it is the time, not the distance, that matters. Much the same is true of food supply. So it is wise to take more than you think you will need even if you expect to arrive at your destination before the next meal-time, or before your supply runs out.

As you travel over the desert sands you feel the fiery heat an hour or two after sunrise and there is no relief until sunset. The fine sand, blown like a spray by the wind, stings the face. But the beauty of the dunes shimmering in the sun makes the trip well worth while. Here the desert is a landscape of curves and infinite variety, like waves of the sea frozen in motion. The windward slopes are gentle gradients, while the leeward slopes drop away steeply. Wherever you turn the waves stretch to the horizon. The surrounding vastness is the vastness of the ocean, but it is an ocean of sand, not water.

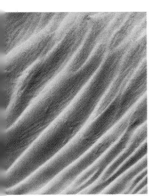

Two detailed photographs of the Saharan desert: top— *furrows in the sand of the erg produced by wind action and resembling veins.* Bottom— *a long view across the Hammada or Rocky desert.*

Imagination . . .

Most people have heard of a mirage and think of it as a vision of something that does not exist. And there are times when the desert traveller may have hallucinations—a vision of a lake or a well or an oasis complete with trees, shadows, human dwellings, or caravans. Such a vision can have all the impact of reality on a person lost in the desert and sick with thirst. He travels on but never finds the place of his imagination. It exists only in his mind and no camera could ever record what he thinks he is seeing.

But there are mirages that are real, visions that are a reflection of reality. What you see is not where you see it—it is somewhere else. But it exists and what you are seeing is the reflection of it. This phenomenon is well known to desert travellers and quite easily explained.

Suppose you are travelling in the desert, say along the border between Algeria and Libya. Suddenly you notice a lake, not far below the horizon. Walking along the undulating line of the sand dunes beyond the lake you see a man with two camels. Man and beasts are walking close to the water's edge and are clearly reflected in the lake. The surface of the lake quivers like a reflection in an antique mirror and its surface appears ruffled as though by a light wind. The sight is convincing because it appears real; yet there is something strange about it.

You scan the map quickly because you cannot recollect a lake in this place. The map convinces you: there is no indication of either a lake or a dried-up lake bed in this vicinity. You take a closer look at what you are seeing and then it dawns on you that what you are looking at is not a real lake at all, but a mirage.

A few minutes later the vision changes. Images previously in sharp focus become blurred as though viewed through a steamed-up lens. It disintegrates and finally disappears. Nothing remains but the reality of sand and dune.

. . . or reality

Presently a man appears in sight

with two camels and you realize that these are the three you saw earlier in the mirage. In the mirage there was a camel in front followed by the man walking with the second camel and this is the position you are seeing them in now. There is no question now that the three figures of the mirage are real, therefore they were real when you saw them earlier.

What causes such a vision of something real that is not there? Such a mirage is caused by the strata of hot and cold air acting as lens and mirror and reflecting an existing image somewhere else. The images you saw really existed and were brought closer to you by reflection. Such a mirage can actually be photographed because the image really exists. It is a reproduction of something real and photographing it might be com-

The optical effect of a mirage in the Central Sahara. Sand dunes and a small caravan are reflected in a mirror of water which does not exist where it is seen. It exists somewhere else and is a reflection of reality, not an hallucination.

pared with photographing a picture in a mirror. The picture does not exist in the mirror; it is merely reflected there. But you can still photograph it.

Berber and Tuareg

Between Morocco on the Atlantic coast and its eastern limits, the great desert is an arid world made up of a variety of peoples. There has been much intermingling and mixing between many tribes, giving rise to a complex of types whose skin colour varies from light to dark.

To meet some of the last of the nomadic tribes is a thrilling and dramatic experience—almost a mirage in itself—a present-day vision of a Saharan world projected from

the distant past. Meeting Berber or Tuareg nomads is an experience like that of the archaeologist who discovers some trace of an ancient civilization that has been buried in the sand for thousands of years.

Berbers and Tuaregs are ancient tribes with a proud history of self sufficiency and victory over the desert, but both are gradually dying out. The Berbers are the nomads of the north; the Tuaregs the nomads of the Central and Southern desert.

The Berbers are shepherds who travel on horseback as was their custom throughout North Africa before the great Arab invasion. For them the horse is a status symbol— a symbol of wealth. They use camels as pack animals and as sources of milk and wool, but they use the horse for riding, and they travel on

A test of courage. Men line up before a group of armed horsemen who approach at a gallop and hurl their spears. The target men most not move and that is the test of their courage. The horsemen have to land their spears close to the men without injuring them and that is the test of their skill.

Armed horsemen approaching the target men.

horseback from village to village.

Berber horsemanship

As a horseman the Berber is usually held in high esteem, but his abilities have been questioned by those qualified to judge the finer points of horsemanship. The main criticisms are that there is a complete lack of sympathy between the Berber and his horse which is for him merely a vehicle. The Berber bridles and bits are severe; his spurs are like daggers.

According to P. Turnbull in his book, *Black Barbary*, "the horse is in such an agony of terror that he will never stretch himself out at full gallop and when urged into a pace faster than a canter by the brutal Berber spurs moves with his head thrown right back. When advancing at a gallop the Berber stands upright in his short stirrups and can turn his horse right or left with the ease and rapidity of a first class polo pony; but this result is attained again by the terrible fierceness of the bitting rather than by expert training."

The Fantasia

The main exhibition of Berber horsemanship is the *fantasia*, and this is a survival of a tradition dating back to the old days when disputes over water rights were common. When several tribes arrived simultaneously at a well the result was an argument about who should take precedence in drawing water and how much should be drawn. Fights took place and blood was often shed. The mountain Berbers of Gaspa agreed to solve the problem of water rights by competition between individuals representing the different tribes gathered at the waterhole. The tribe represented by the winning pair had priority at the waterhole. Being first at drinking time meant abundant clean water, whereas those who came later might find the well nearly dry or muddy because of the number of men, women, and children who had used it.

In the old competition young horsemen lined up on a flat piece of ground, ready to run a course of about one thousand yards between two rows of people made up of all the tribes gathered at the waterhole. At the other end of the track was a line of men buried up to their necks in the sand. Horsemen armed with lances galloped down on the buried men who were their targets. But the test of skill was in scoring near misses, in other words to plant the lance as closely as possible to the head of a man without actually hitting him.

After the first gallop the roles were reversed. The men on horseback were buried in the sand and the men who had been buried now mounted the horses. And so the contest would go on. Each pair, the horseman and the target, represented a tribe.

Nowadays the *fantasia* is a simple charge of horsemen that ends in a festival. Those taking part in the *fantasia* form up on open ground. At a signal they move forward, first at a walk, then at a canter, then at a gallop. As they approach the end of the track the horsemen stand up in their stirrups uttering loud cries and discharging rifles into the air.

As one group of riders leaves the track to take part in the feasting and jubilation another group lines up to charge down the track and fire their rifles. It is a simple display but it still attracts spectators who can watch repeated performances for hours on

The charge of horsemen during a fantasia in the Saharan desert. This rough, riding game is a survival from the days when tournaments were fought over water rights in desert.

end without becoming bored by its repetitiveness.

The *fantasia* takes place in the evening when it is cool, and there is neither wind nor dust to interfere with the proceedings. The light is then soft and men, animals, and objects can be clearly distinguished.

The blue men

The Tuareg, the Blue men of Berber origin, are the most ancient inhabitants of the Sahara. They say of themselves: "We are free men, independent and predatory." And this self-portrait is the only certain fact about their history, which still has not been clearly traced by modern research. The scientist finds difficulty in separating myth and legend from fact.

There have been many theories as to their origin. According to one of these the Tuareg appeared in North Africa about 1000 B.C. Egyptian art of the period represents them as northern Doric types. On the other hand many scholars feel that they are not Doric and that they came from Crete or Asia Minor.

A Bedouin child from an African village.

Whichever of these theories is correct there is no doubt at all that they were incomers like the Lebu, the people from whom Libya took its name. They descended on Africa from the eastern basin of the Mediterranean, crossing from Crete to Cyrenaica and made a vain attempt to settle in the valley of the Nile. Failing to infiltrate the rich land of the Pharaohs they were driven within the frontiers of the Sahara. After a series of migrations, of which nothing is known and about which nothing is now likely to be discovered, this strong resolute people finally settled in the rocky Central Sahara, the area of the Hoggar which is their present-day territory.

The most incredible theory about the origin of the Tuareg is that they came from the legendary Atlantis, escaping from the doomed land before it disappeared under the ocean. Yet another theory, stretching the imagination even further, is that they had a common Atlantic origin with the Aztecs and Incas of South America.

But putting all fantastic theories aside it seems certain that for over three thousand years the Tuareg have been a distinct ethnic group — compact and separate, completely autonomous and unmixed almost to the present day. They have the longest continuous association with the Sahara. Theirs is a saga of lost beginnings, a poetic mythology untouched by a thousand scientific doubts.

Changeless ways

Like their mythology the Tuaregs themselves are changeless. They conquered one of the most hostile desert areas in the world, yet seem unable to adapt to the world of today. Their numbers are dwindling

The Tuareg, or blue men, are the most conservative traditionalists in the desert. Here is the head man of a northern Nigerian Tuareg tribe, photographed with his weapons on the outskirts of Kano. The traditional swords were once forged for the Tuareg leaders by enslaved Negroes known as Iklan. The Tuaregs believed that the Iklan could bring luck to the owner of the weapon by the magic symbols engraved on it.

The Sahara is the biggest desert in the world. It lies between 17° and 34° parallel north, and extends across the entire African continent from the Atlantic to the Red Sea. Its structure is simple and of three distinct types—Erg, or sand dunes; Hammada, or rock desert; and Chott—vast expanses of salt.

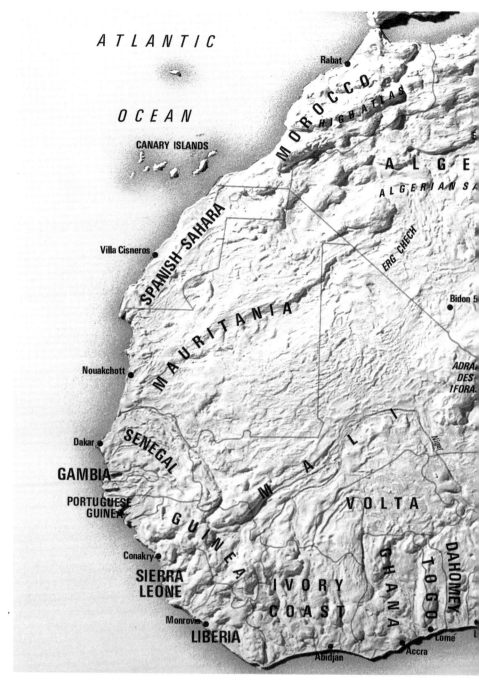

A T L A N T I C

O C E A N

CANARY ISLANDS

MOROCCO

Rabat

HIGH ATLAS

ALGE

ALGERIAN SA

SPANISH SAHARA

Villa Cisneros

ERG CHECH

Bidon 5

MAURITANIA

Nouakchott

ADRA
DES
IFORA.

Niger

Dakar

SENEGAL

GAMBIA

MALI

PORTUGUESE
GUINEA

VOLTA

GUINEA

GHANA

DAHOMEY

Conakry

SIERRA
LEONE

IVORY

TOGO

Monrovia

COAST

Lomé

LIBERIA

Abidjan

Accra

and their destiny may be life on a reservation, like the Indians of North America. Or it may be that the Tuareg as a distinct people may disappear altogether.

The Tuareg are often called Blue Men because of the indigo dye on their skin. The Tuareg male wears cape and turban of indigo blue and these are the source of the dye. The men keep their faces covered all the time, while the women are not veiled at all. They cling to their old caste system and no Tuareg of any status would ever dream of uncovering his face or his nose in the

110

presence of strangers. They cling to their old superstitions and their old marriage customs.

Monogamy is the rule and the women of the Tuareg enjoy a status unequalled in any other part of the Moslem world.

The resistance of the Tuareg to change is almost total, although, as we shall see, he has adopted certain modern methods of hunting. His resistance to education means that the sons of his former slaves are often better educated than he, and therefore able to earn their living in a way he could never do.

The silver cross of Agades—a sacred emblem of the Tuareg.

The Tuareg were once the pirates of the desert, carrying out their raids on swift camels. Although they no longer plunder the caravans and settlements or steal slaves, they are still slave owners. They solved their water problems in a different way from the Berbers, using slaves to draw water for them. Such slaves do all their menial work, and no Tuareg would even think of saddling his own camel. The slaves also raise his crops.

Language and signs

Although the Tuareg are so widely dispersed, and a hundred names have been given to the various groups scattered about the Sahara, they all speak the same language. The "white" tribes of Kel-ajjer can speak to the "black" ones of Kel-azben. This language is called *Tamahak*.

Besides having a common language all the Tuareg have a common cultural heritage—the same myths, the same legends, the same customs and the same religion. In addition to their spoken language the Tuareg have a mute language, a method of communication among themselves that is totally unintelligible to strangers. When they use this means of communication an interviewer is completely at a loss. This method of communication is carried out by hand signals. One man grasps his neighbour's hand and runs his finger over the palm, as though writing words at high speed. In a few seconds the message is conveyed from one man to another and is understood by all without the exchange of a single word.

The system is understood by all men of the same group and is a communal language used by widely separated people, just like the spoken world.

The Tuareg have made one concession to modern living. In the old days they hunted the big desert gazelle, the oryx, with camels and nets. Today they hunt with jeeps instead of camels but they still use the nets.

A modern hunter

Hunting these gazelles can mean

A symbolic combat between two Tuaregs against the Jinn, or evil spirits of the desert. When a group of Tuaregs has decided on a camping place in the desert they drive the evil spirits away from their tents by means of magic formulae and blows of their swords.

hours of tracking. Every six miles or so the hunters get out of their jeeps to examine gazelle droppings. They can tell by looking at them just how old they are, which means they know how far the animals are ahead.

After two or three hours travelling over the monotonous expanse of the hammada one of the guides sitting on the bonnet of the jeep calls out that he has spotted gazelles ahead and points out the direction to the other hunters. The animals are far away and barely distinguishable against the light. They look smaller than they are but this a common illusion in a country of such distant horizons.

The gazelles are running ahead at a speed of about 37 miles an hour and the hunters adjust their speed to keep in contact. As the animals, tiring, begin to slow down the hunters do the same. Eventually the gazelles come to a halt, panting, and exhausted, with nowhere to

seek refuge on the flat expanse of the hammada.

This is the moment the hunters have been waiting for. They carry no rifles, and no weapons—only a net of braided cord in the back of the jeep. This net is taken out, placed on the ground, unwound, stretched between two jeeps and securely anchored to wooden poles. The plan is to drive the animals into the net between the two jeeps using a third jeep as outrider and herder.

The long chase

Now the engines have started up and their roar shatters the silence of the desert. The gazelles become alarmed and they shudder as though from cold. Their ears go up and they mill around nervously. Then, suddenly, they are once more in flight across the hammada.

The jeeps start off after them, the two with the net following in their tracks, the third running alongside

The carefully painted face of a Tuareg woman. She is a member of the Kel Azben tribe of the Southern Sahara in the territory of the Niger. The Tuareg women enjoy a relatively emancipated status.

as herder. The jeeps in the rear must keep the net taut between them, and it must not be allowed to touch the ground or it would rip apart. This calls for considerable driving skill. The hunters now know that one of two things is going to happen: they will either net some gazelles or lose them if a jeep breaks down or the net is torn.

Presently the gazelles slow down again for they are literally out on their feet. One of the hunters lets out a yell and the two drivers increase their speed while the third jeep roars alongside the herd. The animals try to scatter, some to the right and some to the left, but the herding jeep keeps a few in line and presently three beautiful specimens are scooped up in the net where they become inextricably entangled.

Storage places at Medenine in Tunisia used by nomads for storing millet, skins, and wool, until the time is favourable for selling or bartering.

Killing for food

The present method is the same as the old one except that in the old days the nets would have been stretched between two fast camels. Of course the pursuing camels could not match the speed of the gazelles but their endurance was greater, so they were always able to maintain contact.

The old style hunt would sometimes last for days. Each night the Tuaregs and their camels would lie down to rest only a short distance away from the gazelles they were pursuing and the hunt would begin again the following morning.

Provided the hunters had enough food and water they could maintain the pursuit for several days, during which the gazelles were never allowed time to snatch a hasty

bite or seek out a watering place. So as the hunt dragged on the gazelles became weaker from hunger and thirst and their chance of escape became less and less. When they were completely exhausted the entire herd would give up, each animal literally dropping in its tracks. They were then easily netted.

In the modern hunt using jeeps, as in the old style hunt with camels, only the old gazelles are killed for food. Young males and young females are released and allowed to go free to breed. In this way the Tuareg of today, like his forebears, practises his own form of wildlife conservation by using a resource animal wisely. The release of young breeding stock ensures a continuing supply of game. Nursing females captured in the net are milked before release. The meat of the old gazelles and a few bowls of milk are the Tuaregs' profit from the hunt.

Oryx and addax

The gazelle hunted by the Tuareg is the scimitar-horned oryx whose long horns curve backwards. It is a relative of the gemsbok and is yellow and white in colour.

The Arabian oryx, now one of the world's rarest animals, was once found in the Libyan Desert. Evidence in support of this is provided by Egyptian and Nubian tombstones on which these oryxes are represented as domestic animals with ropes round their necks. The ancient Egyptians depicted other antelope species but the oryx was the one most frequently drawn. The Egyptians kept many oryxes. The tombstone of the arch-priest, Sabonna, in Memphis, dating from the beginning of the Fifth dynasty, records that he owned 1,308 oryxes, 1,135 gazelles, and 1,244 addaxes. All these antelopes were kept by the Egyptians, mainly for their meat. The Arabian oryx, as we have seen, is no longer found in Africa and has almost disappeared from Arabia but is being bred in Arizona.

The addax is now becoming rarer in the desert. Formerly it was a common animal in the Tunisian and Algerian Sahara up to Kordofan and southwards in the direction of Senegal and the Chad Lake. The Arabs regard the addax as a noble animal of the chase and hunt it with specially trained dogs. Despite its speed and endurance it rarely escapes.

Nowadays the practice of hunting the addax in motor cars instead of on horseback has speeded up its destruction. By 1900 it had been exterminated in Egypt. Although hunting is prohibited in many African states, it is still carried on illegally. Motor cars can run the addaxes to death because the ground is easy to cover even off the roads.

The addax is a strong, low-set, clumsy antelope with ringed horns slightly twisted in the shape of a lyre. In adult animals the horns form two spirals. The basic colour is yellow and white but the head is brown. There is a white blaze between the eyes and a white spot behind the ears and on the upper lip. The addax stands between three and four feet in overall height.

Kings and chiefs

The king, or local chief, of a Tuareg tribe is known as the Amenokal, which, literally translated, means "owner of the country". In the name Amenokal the prefix *Am* means possession and *kal* means land. Such a title is conferred upon the supreme chief of many tribes as in the Hoggar, or even upon the chief of small groups as in the Sudan or Niger. But al-

Terracotta flasks used by nomads of the Northern Sahara for storing date palm oil.

Tuareg women building a mud hut at the edge of an oasis.

though he has certain formal regal duties the Amenokal's status is solely that of a political chief who is removable from his post.

But despite this system of chiefs and subordinates, or kings and commoners, the Tuareg are not a submissive people and subordination of one to another is not a noticeable characteristic in their relationships. Even among the most rigidly traditional Tuaregs there is never any of the servility to be found in other Arab societies where sultans and princes are accorded exalted status. No Tuareg kneels when his chief passes by, nor prostrates himself before speaking to him. In fact he commits no formal act of submission at any time. In this he resembles the old style clansman of the Scottish Highlands, who always considered himself no better than his chief but was always prepared to concede that his chief might be as good a man as he.

The Amenokal's power is symbolically represented by a large drum. Damage to this drum represents a great injury to his prestige. To abandon it to an enemy, or to lighten a camel's load, or to lose it in a tent fire, is a grave dishonour to the entire community.

Music and poetry

The Tuareg's taste for music and poetry is indulged at night around the camp fire. Tales are told in song, accompanied by a sort of harp played exclusively by women. It is generally the Amenokal himself who sings of the ancient stories and legends of the tribe. The songs are memorized and passed from father to son. These myths and legends constitute the most original part of the Tuareg literature, which is an oral tradition unsurpassed in fantasy and wealth of imagery by that of any other tribe of the Sahara.

The songs tell of legendary Tuareg heroes of the Air and the Hoggar, heroes like Hoggar, Elias, and Alamellen, famous for their

mighty deeds as hunters. Their names live today in the names of the best known and highest peaks of the mountains of the Tuareg country.

Each mountain has been endowed with a precise personality, a body and a soul. The songs tell of one mountain falling in love with another. There is one tale that tells how the Ilaman peak (a rocky spur pointing proudly towards the sky), fell in love with the slender, elegant hill of Tarelrelt. Ilaman was so enamoured of Tarelrelt that he fought for her with a rival, Mount Amga. In this fierce battle Ilaman lost an arm, while his rival Amga was wounded in the side by a lance. From this wound was born a perennial spring that gushes out of the side of Amga to this day.

No one steals from God

If you were in the area of Agadés in Niger you might see a group of Tuareg leaving for the north with their flocks and herds. This is one of their migrations in search of new pastures in the mountains and the valleys of Air. If you travelled with them you would notice that many of the camels carried sacks of millet on their backs. Then, one morning you would wake up and find that the camels were no longer carrying these loads. If you asked the Amenokal for an explanation he would probably make a speech something like this:

"We have hidden the millet in caves in the hills close to the trail we have been travelling. In these caves it will be safe and available to our people on the next journey through during the dry season. The Tuareg will know where to find it because we always use the same storage caves."

If you were to ask the Amenokal if it was safe to leave such precious food supplies unprotected he would probably reply:

"No one steals the millet left under God's protection."

The Amenokal's forefathers had left their millet in these same caves and the Tuareg of today does the same, confident that no one in the desert will ever commit the grave sin of stealing someone else's food even though he might be on the point of death himself. A faith like this is part of the nobility of the Tuareg character, a faith in people, the faith that makes him believe that others will behave like himself.

Power from wind and sun

The strong winds of the Sahara have long been used for driving dynamos to produce power. There are wind-driven power stations where a wind-mill drives the dynamo and the dynamo feeds a battery which produces enough light to supply just one lamp. In some areas there are wind motors on a bigger scale. Some windmills have more vanes and a more complicated system that results in a stream of air driving a turbine that produces up to one hundred kilowatts. This system has a great future in the desert, but although the wind is a more or less constant factor it is also unreliable and in summer a whole crop can be endangered if a wind-driven pump used for irrigation is out of action for only twenty-four hours.

Many scientists are now looking to the sun to help in taming the desert and make conditions less harsh for those who live there. It has been estimated that on an area 60 miles square the sun discharges about 40,000 million kilowatt hours per year. This is greater than the whole world output of electricity. In two and a half million acres of desert solar batteries could be a very important source of energy. If the cost were not too prohibitive, power stations might be built using the sun as their source of energy.

But trapping and utilizing solar energy is expensive.

Many scientists, studying the problem of energy in the desert, are looking to the atom for the answer and small atomic power plants may yet play an important part in the Sahara's future. But it may be a long time before atomic energy becomes a cheap source of power.

To make the desert a garden

Although men constantly dream of turning the Sahara into a productive garden, such dreams are still a long way from being realized. To increase life in the desert means increasing its supply of energy and the ultimate source of energy for all higher organisms is an increase in plant life. Of course plants already grow in the desert but they are scarce and of a few species adapted to the extremes of climate and shortage of water.

Hollows in the northern plains are sometimes bright with purple iris after a shower of rain. Here and there bushes with scarlet fruits brighten the sands. The nomads know where to find vegetation in the desert and such knowledge is vital to their existence, for they need forage for their camels and sheep as well as food for themselves and fuel for their camp fires. In addition to this the desert plants supply the nomads with medicines, cosmetics and dyes. The known areas of vegetation, besides providing food, act as guideposts to the nomads over the trackless sand.

How much can science help to irrigate the land and produce larger numbers of plants? How much water can be provided from underground reservoirs? The discovery of large reservoirs of fresh water under 600 feet high dunes in the Sahara has caused great excitement and optimism, and field crews are already exploring various sites with instruments to find places that could be drilled profitably. It has been estimated that the world's largest single reservoir of fresh water lies under the sand of Western Egypt.

Water by technology

In some areas water is already being pumped from beneath the desert twenty-four hours a day. Large numbers of animals, bawling and bickering for the water that was once so scarce, come to the new waterholes to slake their thirst. Camels drink their fill, gulping down many gallons of water at once. But the scientist has to do more than provide enough water to quench the thirst of camels. He is still faced with the challenge of finding enough water to irrigate vast areas of desert so that more people can enjoy the comfort of ample water over a larger area than ever before. Nevertheless, a small beginning has been made in supplying the needs of the thirsty Sahara.

Another approach to solving the water problem is the building of dams. This is a conservation problem—the storage of water that is already there. The largest of these dams is the Aswan in Egypt, which is 436 feet high and 2.6 miles long.

Rocks broken apart by heat in the heart of the Sahara on the border between the Niger and Southern Algeria.

The Aswan dam stores the waters of the Nile and is estimated to have seventeen times the volume of the Cheops Great Pyramid. It will eventually irrigate about two million acres of desert land.

It has been said that Egypt has to run in order to stand still because the population is increasing so fast. By the creation of two million acres of extra irrigated land, the green strip along the Nile will be widened to supply food for the greater number of mouths that must now be fed.

Many problems have to be met and overcome before dams like the Aswan, or even smaller ones, can be built. For instance, mountains had to be blasted at Aswan and literally shifted to block the flow of the Nile. Whole villages had to be cleared and the people housed elsewhere. Twenty-six Nubian villages are now under water. The people of these villages were provided with new homes but for many of them the move was an unhappy one and there were even some who wanted to remain behind, even though their villages were about to be inundated.

A Bedouin woman and her boy photographed at an oasis near oil drillings. Both are wrapped in black cloaks.

Saving the treasures

A world-wide effort enabled the engineers to save the Abu Simbel temples built by the ancient Egyptians along the banks of the Nile. The temples were dismantled and rebuilt at a higher level, work that involved hewing great blocks from the rock and shifting them entire. A block weighing 25 tons was raised about seventy yards. By this effort famous monuments have been preserved.

A number of other archaeological treasures were also rescued from the Nile, but many monuments of lesser value now lie under the water of the largest man-made reservoir in the world—Lake Nasser. A diversion channel has been dug and the course of the Nile has been diverted from its original path into twelve tunnels hewn in solid granite. A power station has been built above the tunnels where turbines generate electricity for Cairo and small industries in Upper Egypt.

Reafforestation

Irrigation on an increasing scale will help to hold back the slow, relentless march of the sand dunes. Sand blown by the wind has been enlarging desert areas and in some parts of the world has engulfed farms and forests, villages and towns. If sand can be held in place on the dunes, plants can be anchored and will draw on the store of water deeper down. But in normal situations the constant movement of sand prevents young trees from taking hold. Scientists are trying to solve this problem of anchoring plants by spraying the sand dunes with oil. This makes the grains of sand cling together so that they can resist the wind and stay in place for some time.

In Tunisia and Libya there are now active programmes of reafforestation. Here the Esso Research and Engineering Company has helped with detailed studies of sand dune behaviour and by the planting of tree seedlings on prepared dunes. The young trees were therefore stabilized until they had a chance to grow. In one experiment eucalyptus seedlings grew to a height of more than 6 feet within a year and were 25 feet high in five years. Long before this the oil had disappeared and the trees were able to stabilize themselves.

Several thousand acres have been sprayed and planted. Not only has

the destructive shifting of sands been halted by this method—the nation hopes, in about fifteen year's time, to harvest a valuable timber crop from trees grown on dunes stabilized by this technique.

Hard experience has shown that experiments like this must be carried out under natural conditions because trees that grew well in the laboratory failed completely when planted outside.

There is another source of water in the desert whose significance is a recent discovery. The Israeli scientist, Shmuel Duvidevani, found that in some areas the dewfall could equal ten inches of rain a year. He also found out that except in extreme desert country, dew could be as heavy in arid lands as in coastal regions. This might account for the fact that crops growing close to the ground, like water melons, could do well in areas of extremely low rainfall. Research into dew may yet increase yields in areas where there is not enough water for proper irrigation. It begins to look as though many plants and animals of the desert have used dew to supply part of their water needs in a way hardly suspected until now.

An achievement and a warning

Israel has been notable for transforming desert lands into productive acres by irrigation. In the words of Walter C. Lowdermilk:

"The example of Israel shows that the land can be reclaimed and that increase in the food supply can overtake the population increase that will double the 2,800 million world population before the end of the century. Israel is a pilot area for the arid lands of the world, especially those of her Arab neighbours who persist in their destitution in the same landscape that Israel has brought into blossom."

But a word of warning comes from the great American, Starker Leopold, who has observed:

"Many of the deep wells being drilled today in deserts around the world are tapping water that can never be replaced. In parts of Baja California, and Sonora, short-term

Arabs and their camel beside an encampment of modern caravans belonging to a field survey geological unit searching for oil in the Central Sahara. Here again, the ancient and the modern can be seen side by side.

121

A jeep pulls up on the edge of a salty lake in Chott Djerid in the Northern Sahara. Before the discovery of iron, copper, magnesium, and oil, salt was the sole mineral resource of this desert. Today it is still one of the exchange goods used by the nomads.

farming projects are being undertaken in the most unpromising creosote-bush desert, based on wells with a probable life span of only ten to fifteen years. The mining of deep water deposits for such temporary production may be no worse than the extraction of irreplaceable minerals and oil from the earth, but it can hardly be looked upon as agricultural progress. The long-term big scale well water irrigation, including Israel's programme, will depend on what permanent changes are wrought in the water sources."

The salt desert

The desert of Chott is salt and looks like an Antarctic landscape. It is a rock desert like an ice field and there is a lake in its central basin. It is the only lake for many miles around and is so heavily laden with mineral salts that no one dare drink from it. Even desert animals do not come to this dead world. The desert of Chott is a desert within a desert in spite of the presence of water.

In the Chott desert about twenty seismographic surveys are made each day and there are lines of exploration stretching for approximately 125 miles. These lines are drawn on topographical maps of the region. When one line has been explored the men start on another until the entire area has been covered. It takes two years of non-stop work to complete a programme of this kind. The work goes on each day whatever the weather or time of year.

Oil wells have never before been drilled in desert regions so far from the sea, not even in Arabia, and never under such difficult conditions. In the Chott desert, in December, the vapour from the turbines freezes on the sounding

line. In July the water evaporates from the cisterns and the radiators. When the temperature is 55 degrees Centigrade in the shade the flies seek out human sweat to survive. In extremes of freezing and heat the work goes on from December to December, stopping only on Christmas Day. The men work in shifts round the clock. The sound of diesel engines never ceases. It is as constant as the wind that blows through the camp, laden with the desert's dust and sand. Supplies for the workers are dropped from the air. Every necessity of life arrives in this way, from water to salad.

Here, in this hostile desolation, workers of different tribes and cultures and backgrounds have to live and work together and their adaptability has been astounding. Proud local tribesmen have to undergo a complete personality change and

Many of today's Saharan nomads have found work in the oil camps of the desert and have thus been released from age-old poverty. The photograph shows a Bedouin driving a modern tracked vehicle.

bend to work they were once too proud to perform. Once they have overcome their reservations about menial tasks they learn how to handle mechanical instruments. The European worker, long familiar with industrial processes and mechanical devices, also changes his outlook when he discovers that the men of the Sahara have much to teach him, not least the patience and endurance that are the hallmarks of the nomad. The European gains from the desert nomad something of the precious knowledge that comes only to those who have lived and died close to nature.

The discovery of oil in the desert has dramatically changed the lives of the desert peoples. Already many nomadic tribes have taken work in the oil camps and settled down nearby. Here there is a great babble of languages—of different tribes and people from other parts of the world. Month after month more and more people settle to work in the oil fields and the nomads of yesterday now work in one place, earning their living from oil. Oil is now flowing from the Sahara in larger quantities than ever before and the search for more oil fields goes on. Modern caravans scour the sun-scorched desert for this black gold and oil is now being piped to many coasts far from the wells from which it gushes.

The developed desert

The transformation of the Sahara is just beginning, not only by the discovery of a great wealth of natural resources but by the consequences of such discoveries.

Trails have become highways. Trucks now travel where only camels used to be seen. New centres of population have grown up where people are learning modern tech-

niques. Thousands of new jobs have become available. Hospitals and schools have been built. Nomadism is decreasing and the agricultural products of the oases have a wider market and greater value than ever before.

A communication network is opening up a land that has been closed for thousands of years, and as a result the men of the desert are being drawn closer to the rest of the world. The world in turn begins to look to the deserts for help, for here is potential living space for exploding populations. Here lies a source of agricultural land that could feed vast numbers of people. Here lies a wealth of mineral resources just beginning to be tapped. In addition to oil there are large deposits of iron, manganese, phosphates, cobalt and other minerals mixed with or lying underneath the desert sands. These are being mined in ever increasing quantities. Projects continue to multiply and a better future awaits the new generations of desert peoples.

In the fifth century B.C., the Greek historian, Herodotus, described in the following words the end of the peoples of Psylli in the Libyan Desert:

"The wind of the south had dried up their cisterns and all the cultivated lands in the Sirte were without water. The leaders then decided to seek a new way out against the wind. But at the moment of crossing the sands the wind buried the entire population."

Today, twenty-five centuries later, other people are seeking new roads across the desert and battling against the wind and the engulfing sands. But neither wind, nor sand, nor heat, nor cold, can stop them. The desert cannot bury them. Instead it is they who are transforming the desert for the future.

A field party with pumping unit and spray treats the sand dunes with oil to stabilize them for the planting of trees. This is one of the methods now being used in the reafforestation of the dunes, which in itself is an attempt to rehabilitate the desert habitat.

After stabilization the dunes are dotted with green bushes. As a result of tree planting, humidity increases, and as humidity increases cultivation can be attempted. In the constant struggle between man and the desert, reafforestation is one of the techniques now used to help make the desert bloom. The realization of this dream may yet be a long way off, but for many parts of the desert a new future has already begun.

FURTHER READING

The Desert by A. Starker Leopold. Time-Life International 1963
The Life of the Desert by Ann and Myron Sutton. McGraw-Hill Book Company 1966
Portrait of a Desert by Guy Mountfort. Collins 1965
South Africa by Tom Hopkinson. Time-Life International 1965

Egypt by Alfred Nawrath. Kümmerly and Frey (Berne)
Journey to the Red Rock by Bruce and June MacPherson. Collins 1965
Children of the Kalahari by Alice Mertens. Collins 1966
The Future of Arid Lands by G. F. White. Bailey Bros. 1956
Animal Life in Deserts by P. A. Buxton. Edward Arnold Ltd. 1923
Locusts and Grasshoppers by B. P. Uvarov. Imperial Bureau of Entomology. London 1928
Quest in the Desert by Roy Chapman Andrews. Viking 1956
Tribes of the Sahara by Lloyd Cabot Briggs. Oxford University Press 1960
Sahara: The Great Desert by E. F. Gautier. University Press 1935

INDEX

Grass, porcupine, 71
Grasshopper, 17
Greasewood, 82
Great Basin, desert, 82, 87
Great Mosque, 28
Gypsum, 82

H
Hammada, 96, 97, 102, 110, 113
Harappa, 49, 51, 52, 54
Hart Mountain National Antelope Refuge, Oregon, 89
Hawk, 38
Hejaz, desert, 24, 26, 28, 29, 30, 34
Herodotus (*c.* 485–425 B.C.), Greek historian, 124
Himalayas, 45
Hindu Kush, 42, 45, 58
Hogan, 84–5
Hoggar, 108, 115, 116; mountains, 93, 97
Hopi. *See* Indians
Horse, 52, 54, 61, 62, 65, 66, 105, 106; Przewalsky's, 65–6
Hottentot, 14, 16
Howitt, William (1792–1879), English author and explorer, 73

I
India, 45, 47, 49, 56, 58; desert of, 24, 45, 55, 81
Indians, 14, 70, 83, 84, 91, 110; sand paintings, 84, 86
Indo-Pakistan desert, 49, 56
Indus, civilization, 47, 49, 51, 52, 57, 58; river, 49, 52; valley, 53
Iran, 30, 35, 38, 39, 41, 45, 54, 59, 67; desert of, 37
Iraq, 24, 35, 36, 55, 66
Iron, 79, 93, 122, 124
Irrigation, 55, 118. *See* also water; canals, 49, 52, 55, 84
Islam, 26, 28; architecture, 25
Israel, 55, 121, 123

J
Jaipur, 46, 47, 50
Jidda, 27, 28
Jordan, 38, desert of, 24, 25, 27; Hollow, 24, 25, 38

K
Kainj. *See* Kulan
Kalahari desert, 13–21, 26, 70
Kanats, 54
Kangaroo, 69, 77
Kangaroo rat, 88, 89–90
Kansu, 61
Kara-Kum, 40
Kathiawar, massacre at, 48, 49, 51, 52
Kazakhstan, 63
Khorosan, 30, 39
Khyber Pass, 42, 45
Kit fox, 88
Kulan, 66; Chigetai, 66; Kainj, 66; Onegar, 66
Kuru, desert, 21
Kuwait, 24, 35, 38

L
Lead, 79
Leopold, Starker, 26, 121
Levant, The, 29
Libya, 93, 94, 96, 100, 108, 120
Libyan desert, 93, 115, 124
Limestone, 23
Lion, 56, 57, 58, 60, 61, 62, 63

Livingstone, David (1813–73), Scottish missionary and explorer, 13
Lizard, 17, 38, 87, 89, 90
Lomas, 91
Los Angeles zoo, 38

M
Mali, 93, 100
Manchuria, 67
Manganese, 93, 124
Mantis, man, 17; praying, 17, 19
Marco Polo (1254–1324), Venetian traveller, 45, 58, 62
Marsupial mole, 77
Mauritania, 93
Mecca, 26, 27, 28, 29, 30; pilgrimage to, 27, 28
Mediterranean sea, 24, 45, 93
Mesquite, 88, 90
Meteorology stations, 93
Mirage, 102–3
Mohammed (570–632), 25, 26, 29
Mohenjo Dharo, 49, 52, 54, 57, 58
Mojave desert, 81
Mongolia, 58, 59, 61, 62, 63, 64, 65, 66, 67
Mongols, 40
Monument Valley, 83, 84
Morocco, 25, 28, 93, 104
Moslems, 27, 28, 30
Mound springs, 74
Mushatta, 25
Myxomatosis, 74

N
Namib desert, 20
Nasser, Lake, 120
National Audubon Society, 89
Navajo. *See* Indians
Navigation, 58, 96, 100
Nefud, desert of, 23, 24, 28, 29, 30, 34
Negeve desert, 55
Nepal, 66
Nevada, 82, 89
New Mexico, 11, 82, 84
Ngami, Lake, 13
Niger, 93, 113, 115, 117, 119
Nigeria, 93
Nile, river, 23, 38, 108, 120
Nomads, 19, 28, 29, 30, 35, 39, 42, 43, 45, 49, 55, 56, 57, 63, 67, 70, 79, 94, 95, 96, 98, 100, 101, 105, 114, 115, 118, 122, 123, 124
Northern Native Territories, 14
Nubian desert, 94
Nullarbor plain, 78

O
Oasis, 26, 30, 34, 39, 46, 49, 96, 98, 99, 120, 124
Oil, 10, 35, 36, 37, 38, 71, 94, 98, 120, 121, 122, 123, 124, 125
Omayad, castle of, 27
Onegar. *See* Kulan
Oregon, 82
Oryx, 20, 37, 38–9, 112–15
Ostrich, egg shells, 20
Oswell, William C., 13
Owl, 38; Screech, 90
Ox, 61, 66

P
Pacific Ocean, 28, 58, 87, 91
Painted desert, 89
Pakistan, 42, 45, 47, 49, 54, 81; West, 52, 81
Palace of the Wind, 47, 50

Pallas, Peter Simon (1741–1811), German-born naturalist, 64
Patagonian desert, 91
Persia, 24, 64, 66
Persian Gulf, 24, 35
Peru, 88; current, 91; desert of, 89, 91
Petroleum, 59, 93, 94, 100
Philippine islands, 28
Phoenix zoo, 38
Phosphates, 93, 124
Platinum, 93
Poison, arrows, 17, 18, 20; snake, 17
Pontok mountains, 17
Prickly pear. *See* Cacti
Pronghorn. *See* Antelope
Przewalsky, Nikolai (1839–88), Russian traveller, 62, 63, 65, 66
Purplemat, 88

Q
Qala, 38, 39, 40
Quanat, or foggara, 40, 41, 42, 54

R
Rabbit, 74
Rainfall, 45, 53, 73, 74, 77, 81, 91, 93; annual, 7
Rajasthan, 45, 46, 48, 50, 52
Rajput, 45, 46, 48; warriors, 48, 49, 51, 52
Rat, 90; Wood, 91
Raven, 38
Red Sea, 23, 27, 93, 110
Rocky mountains, 82, 85
Rub'al Khali, 23, 24, 30
Russia. *See* U.S.S.R.

S
Sagebrush, 82, 87
Saguaro. *See* Cacti
Sahara desert, 7, 41, 69, 70, 75, 81, 91, 93–125; Spanish, 93
Saiga, 63–4
Salt, 82, 87, 96
Saltbush, 71, 82
Sand, 55, 93, 99, 102, 124; "drums of the dunes", 94–6; dunes, 7, 20, 26, 37, 52, 73, 81, 82, 87, 94, 97, 103, 110, 120, 121, 125; sandstone, 23, 24, 74, 75
Sand grouse, 38
Saudi Arabia, 24, 26, 30, 35, 38
Scorpion, 17, 21; men, 17, 18
Sheep, 39, 42, 61, 63, 74, 77, 94, 118; Bighorn, 89; stations, 70, 74
Sheldon, Charles Sheldon Antelope Refuge of Nevada, 89
Sierra Nevada, 82
Silver, 79
Sinai, 38
Sind desert, 45, 47, 49, 52, 53, 54, 56, 57, 59
Sioux. *See* Indians
Skink, Hungarian, 38
Snake, 17, 38, 91
Somalia, 30
Sonora desert, 81, 91, 121
Soviet Union. *See* U.S.S.R.
Spain, 25; Rock paintings, 17; Sahara, 93
Sparrowhawk, 90
Spider, 17, 21
Spinifax, 71
Stuart, John McDouall (1815–66), Scottish-born Australian explorer, 73
Sturt, Charles (1795–1869), British explorer, 71
Sudan, 30, 93, 115
Syria, 26, 66; desert of, 27

ACKNOWLEDGEMENTS

David Muench, 6, 11, 80, 83, 85
Joseph Muench, 86
Richard Jepperson-APA, 87
SEF, 17, 26, 27, 38, 39

Folco Quilici, 15, 15, 16, 18, 19, 20, 21, 22, 29, 30, 31, 32, 33, 33, 33, 34, 35, 42, 43, 43, 44, 46, 48, 49, 49, 50, 51, 52, 53, 55, 56, 59, 60, 61, 62, 63, 87, 91, 91, 91, 92, 95, 96, 96, 97, 98, 98, 99, 100, 100, 101, 103, 104, 106, 106, 107, 108, 109, 112, 113, 114, 119, 120, 122, 123
Grassetti, 28, 28, 40, 46, 54, 54, 59, 94, 94, 109, 112, 115
Total, 36, 36, 37, 121
Fiore, 56

Prato, 57, 58, 68, 102, 102
Baglin, 13, 70, 71, 72, 74, 75, 76, 77, 78
Cascio, 88
Esso, 125, 125
Mandel, 25
Cirani, 40
Micheli, 64, 66, 67
Crocellà, 34, 90